WORDS ON A JOURNEY

WORDS ON A JOURNEY

THE GREAT SPEECHES OF PRESIDENT-ELECT BARACK OBAMA

SPECIAL INAUGURATION EDITION

ARC
MANOR
Rockville, MARYLAND
2009

WORDS ON A JOURNEY: THE GREAT SPEECHES OF PRESIDENT-ELECT BARACK OBAMA (SPECIAL INAUGURATION EDITION) has been compiled from various sources, including material provided by the Barack Obama Campaign, the Democratic National Committee and the Republican National Committee.

The original text has been reformatted for clarity and to fit this edition.

Arc Manor, Arc Manor Classic Reprints, Manor Classics, TARK Classic Fiction, and the Arc Manor and TARK Classic Fiction logos are trademarks or registered trademarks of Arc Manor Publishers, Rockville, Maryland. All other trademarks are properties of their respective owners. Arc Manor is an independent publisher and is not associated with any governmental or political entity.

This book is presented as is, without any warranties (implied or otherwise) as to the accuracy of the production, text or translation. The publisher does not take responsibility for any typesetting, formatting, translation or other errors which may have occurred during the production of this book.

ISBN: 978-1-60450-426-2

Published by Arc Manor
P. O. Box 10339
Rockville, MD 20849-0339
www.ArcManor.com
Printed in the United States of America/United Kingdom

Contents

The 2008 Presidential Election

November 4, 2008

BARACK OBAMA
66.8 Million Votes (53%)
365 Electoral Votes

JOHN MCCAIN
58.3 Million Votes (46%)
173 Electoral Votes

A Brief Chronology

August 4, 1961: Barack Hussein Obama, Jr. born in Honolulu, Hawai'i.

1983: Obama graduates from Columbia College, Columbia University.

1985: Obama moves to Chicago and is hired as director of the Developing Communities Project (DCP), a church-based community organization.

1988: Obama joins Harvard Law School.

1989: Obama meets Michelle Robinson at the Chicago law firm of Sidley Austin.

1990: Obama is chosen as the president of the Harvard Law Review. He is the first black president of the prestigious journal.

1991: Obama finishes his studies at the Harvard Law School.

1992: Obama directs Illinois 'Project Vote' (a voter registration drive) from April to October.

1992: Michelle and Obama marry.

1995: *Dreams From My Father* (Obama's first memoir) published.

1995: Obama launches his first run for the Illinois Senate.

1996: Obama elected to the Illinois State Senate.

1998: Malia Ann Obama (daughter) born.

2000: Obama loses the Democratic Primary for the U.S. House of Representatives.

2000: Obama unable to get on the floor of the 2000 Democratic National Convention (and his credit cards do not have sufficient unused credit to rent a car).

2001: Natasha Obama (daughter, Sasha) born.

2003. Obama becomes the chairman of the Illinois Senate's Health and Human Service Committee.

2003: Obama announces his candidacy for the U.S. Senate.

2004: Obama delivers the keynote address at the 2004 Democratic National Convention.

2004: Obama elected to the U.S. Senate.

2006: *The Audacity of Hope* (the second book by Obama) is published.

February 10, 2008: Obama announces his candidacy for the President of the United States.

January 3, 2008: Obama wins the Iowa Caucus

June 3, 2008: Obama achieves sufficient wins in the Democratic Primary to become the 'presumptive' Democratic presidential nominee.

August 25, 2008: Obama becomes the official 2008 Nominee of the Democratic Party.

November 4, 2008: Senator Barack Obama decisively defeats Senator John McCain to become the President Elect of the United States. Obama wins 53% of the popular vote and 365 Electoral Votes (McCain wins 46% of the popular vote and 173 Electoral Votes).

January 20, 2009. Inauguration Day. Barack Obama expected to be sworn in as the 44th President of the United States.

Key Speeches of
President-Elect Barack Obama
44th President of the
United States

Illinois State Senator Barack Obama:

Speech Against Going to War With Iraq

October 2, 2002

*G*ood afternoon. Let me begin by saying that although this has been billed as an anti-war rally, I stand before you as someone who is not opposed to war in all circumstances. The Civil War was one of the bloodiest in history, and yet it was only through the crucible of the sword, the sacrifice of multitudes, that we could begin to perfect this union, and drive the scourge of slavery from our soil. I don't oppose all wars.

My grandfather signed up for a war the day after Pearl Harbor was bombed, fought in Patton's army. He saw the dead and dying across the fields of Europe; he heard the stories of fellow troops who first entered Auschwitz and Treblinka. He fought in the name of a larger freedom, part of that arsenal of democracy that triumphed over evil, and he did not fight in vain. I don't oppose all wars.

After September 11th, after witnessing the carnage and destruction, the dust and the tears, I supported this administration's pledge to hunt down and root out those who would slaughter innocents in the name of intolerance, and I would willingly take up arms myself to prevent such tragedy from happening again. I don't oppose all wars. And I know that in this crowd today, there is no shortage of patriots, or of patriotism.

What I am opposed to is a dumb war. What I am opposed to is a rash war. What I am opposed to is the cynical attempt by Richard Perle and Paul Wolfowitz and other armchair, weekend warriors in this administration to shove their own ideological agendas down our throats, irrespective of the costs in lives lost and in hardships borne.

What I am opposed to is the attempt by political hacks like Karl Rove to distract us from a rise in the uninsured, a rise in the poverty rate, a drop in the median income—to distract us from corporate scandals and a stock market that has just gone through the worst month since the Great Depression. That's what I'm opposed to. A dumb war. A rash war. A war based not on reason but on passion, not on principle but on politics. Now let me be clear—I suffer no illusions about Saddam Hussein. He is a brutal man. A ruthless man. A man who butchers his own people to secure his own power. He has repeatedly defied UN resolutions, thwarted UN inspection teams, developed chemical and biological weapons, and coveted nuclear capacity. He's a bad guy. The world, and the Iraqi people, would be better off without him.

But I also know that Saddam poses no imminent and direct threat to the United States, or to his neighbors, that the Iraqi economy is in shambles, that the Iraqi military a fraction of its former strength, and that in concert with the international community he can be contained until, in the way of all petty dictators, he falls away into the dustbin of history. I know that even a successful war against Iraq will require a US occupation of undetermined length, at undetermined cost, with undetermined consequences. I know that an invasion of Iraq without a clear rationale and without strong international support will only fan the flames of the Middle East, and encourage the worst, rather than best, impulses of the Arab world, and strengthen the recruitment arm of Al Qaeda. I am not opposed to all wars. I'm opposed to dumb wars.

So for those of us who seek a more just and secure world for our children, let us send a clear message to the President today. You want a fight, President Bush? Let's finish the fight with Bin Laden and Al Qaeda, through effective, coordinated intelligence, and a shutting down of the financial networks that support terrorism, and a homeland security program that involves more than color-coded warnings. You want a fight, President Bush?

Let's fight to make sure that the UN inspectors can do their work, and that we vigorously enforce a non-proliferation treaty, and that former enemies and current allies like Russia safeguard and ultimately eliminate their stores of nuclear material, and that nations like Pakistan and India never use the terrible weapons already in their possession, and that the arms merchants in our own country stop feeding the countless wars that rage across the globe. You want a fight, President Bush?

Let's fight to make sure our so-called allies in the Middle East, the Saudis and the Egyptians, stop oppressing their own people, and suppressing dissent, and tolerating corruption and inequality, and mismanaging their economies so that their youth grow up without education, without prospects, without hope, the ready recruits of terrorist cells. You want a fight, President Bush? Let's fight to wean ourselves off Middle East oil, through an energy policy that doesn't simply serve the interests of Exxon and Mobil. Those are the battles that we need to fight. Those are the battles that we willingly join. The battles against ignorance and intolerance. Corruption and greed. Poverty and despair.

The consequences of war are dire, the sacrifices immeasurable. We may have occasion in our lifetime to once again rise up in defense of our freedom, and pay the wages of war. But we ought not—we will not—travel down that hellish path blindly. Nor should we allow those who would march off and pay the ultimate sacrifice, who would prove the full measure of devotion with their blood, to make such an awful sacrifice in vain.

Illinois Senator Barack Obama: Keynote Address at the 2004 Democratic National Convention

July 27, 2004

*O*n behalf of the great state of Illinois, crossroads of a nation, land of Lincoln, let me express my deep gratitude for the privilege of addressing this convention. Tonight is a particular honor for me because, let's face it, my presence on this stage is pretty unlikely. My father was a foreign student, born and raised in a small village in Kenya. He grew up herding goats, went to school in a tin-roof shack. His father, my grandfather, was a cook, a domestic servant.

But my grandfather had larger dreams for his son. Through hard work and perseverance my father got a scholarship to study in a magical place: America, which stood as a beacon of freedom and opportunity to so many who had come before. While studying here, my father met my mother. She was born in a town on the other side of the world, in Kansas. Her father worked on oil rigs and farms through most of the Depression. The day after Pearl Harbor he signed up for duty, joined Patton's army and marched across Europe. Back home, my grandmother raised their baby and went to work on a bomber assembly line. After the war, they studied on the GI Bill, bought a house through FHA, and moved west in search of opportunity.

And they, too, had big dreams for their daughter, a common dream, born of two continents. My parents shared not only an improbable love; they shared an abiding faith in the possibilities of this nation. They would give me an African name, Barack, or "blessed," believing that in a tolerant America your name is no barrier to success. They imagined me going to the best schools in the land, even though they weren't rich, because in a generous America you don't have to be rich to achieve your potential. They are both passed away now. Yet, I know that, on this night, they look down on me with pride.

I stand here today, grateful for the diversity of my heritage, aware that my parents' dreams live on in my precious daughters. I stand here knowing that my story is part of the larger American story, that I owe a debt to all of those who came before me, and that, in no other country on earth, is my story even possible. Tonight, we gather to affirm the greatness of our nation, not because of the height of our skyscrapers, or the power of our military, or the size of our economy. Our pride is based on a very simple premise, summed up in a declaration made over two hundred years ago, "We hold these truths to he self-evident, that all men are created equal. That they are endowed by their Creator with certain inalienable rights. That among these are life, liberty and the pursuit of happiness."

That is the true genius of America, a faith in the simple dreams of its people, the insistence on small miracles. That we can tuck in our children at night and know they are fed and clothed and safe from harm. That we can say what we think, write what we think, without hearing a sudden knock on the door. That we can have an idea and start our own business without paying a bribe or hiring somebody's son. That we can participate in the political process without fear of retribution, and that our votes will he counted—or at least, most of the time.

This year, in this election, we are called to reaffirm our values and commitments, to hold them against a hard reality and see how we are measuring up, to the legacy of our forbearers, and the promise of future generations. And fellow Americans—Democrats, Republicans, Independents—I say to you tonight: we have more work to do. More to do for the workers I met in Galesburg, Illinois, who are losing their union jobs at the Maytag plant that's moving to Mexico, and now are having to compete with their own children for jobs that pay seven bucks an hour. More to do for the father I met who was losing his job and choking back tears, wondering how he would pay $4,500 a month for the drugs his son needs without the health benefits he counted on. More to do for the young woman in East St. Louis, and thousands more like her, who has the grades, has the drive, has the will, but doesn't have the money to go to college.

Don't get me wrong. The people I meet in small towns and big cities, in diners and office parks, they don't expect government to solve all their problems. They know they have to work hard to get ahead and they want to. Go into the collar counties around Chicago, and people will tell you they don't want their tax money wasted by a welfare agency or the Pentagon. Go into any inner city neighborhood, and folks will tell you that government alone can't teach kids to learn. They know that parents have to parent, that children can't achieve unless we raise their expectations and turn off the television sets and eradicate the slander that says a black youth with a book is acting white. No, people don't expect government to solve all their problems. But they sense, deep in their bones, that with just a change in priorities, we can make sure that every child in America has a decent shot at life, and that the doors of opportunity remain open to all. They know we can do better. And they want that choice.

In this election, we offer that choice. Our party has chosen a man to lead us who embodies the best this country has to offer. That man is John Kerry. John Kerry understands the ideals of community, faith, and sacrifice, because they've defined his life. From his heroic service in Vietnam to his years as prosecutor and lieutenant governor, through two decades in the United States Senate, he has devoted himself to this country. Again and again, we've seen him make tough choices when easier ones were available. His values and his record affirm what is best in us.

John Kerry believes in an America where hard work is rewarded. So instead of offering tax breaks to companies shipping jobs overseas, he'll offer them to companies creating jobs here at home. John Kerry believes in an America where all Americans can afford the same health coverage our politicians in Washington have for themselves. John Kerry believes in energy independence, so we aren't held hostage to the profits of oil companies or the sabotage of foreign oil fields. John Kerry believes in the constitutional freedoms that have made our country the envy of the world, and he will never sacrifice our basic liberties nor use faith as a wedge to divide us. And John Kerry believes that in a dangerous world, war must be an option, but it should never he the first option.

A while back, I met a young man named Shamus at the VFW Hall in East Moline, Illinois. He was a good-looking kid, six-two or six-three, clear-eyed, with an easy smile. He told me he'd joined the Marines and was heading to Iraq the following week. As I listened to him explain why he'd enlisted, his absolute faith in our country and its leaders, his devotion to duty and service, I thought this young man was all any of us might hope for in a child. But then I asked myself: Are we serving Shamus as well as he was serving us? I thought of more than 900 service men and women, sons and daughters, husbands and wives, friends and neighbors, who will not be returning to their hometowns. I thought of families I had met who were struggling to get by without a loved one's full income, or whose loved ones had returned with a limb missing or with nerves shattered, but who still lacked long-term health benefits because they were reservists. When we send our young men and women into harm's way, we have a solemn obligation not to fudge the numbers or shade the truth about why they're going, to care for their families while they're gone, to tend to the soldiers upon their return, and to never ever go to war without enough troops to win the war, secure the peace, and earn the respect of the world.

Now let me be clear. We have real enemies in the world. These enemies must be found. They must be pursued and they must be defeated. John

Kerry knows this. And just as Lieutenant Kerry did not hesitate to risk his life to protect the men who served with him in Vietnam, President Kerry will not hesitate one moment to use our military might to keep America safe and secure. John Kerry believes in America. And he knows it's not enough for just some of us to prosper. For alongside our famous individualism, there's another ingredient in the American saga.

A belief that we are connected as one people. If there's a child on the south side of Chicago who can't read, that matters to me, even if it's not my child. If there's a senior citizen somewhere who can't pay for her prescription and has to choose between medicine and the rent, that makes my life poorer, even if it's not my grandmother. If there's an Arab American family being rounded up without benefit of an attorney or due process, that threatens my civil liberties. It's that fundamental belief—I am my brother's keeper, I am my sister's keeper—that makes this country work. It's what allows us to pursue our individual dreams, yet still come together as a single American family. "E pluribus unum." Out of many, one.

Yet even as we speak, there are those who are preparing to divide us, the spin masters and negative ad peddlers who embrace the politics of anything goes. Well, I say to them tonight, there's not a liberal America and a conservative America—there's the United States of America. There's not a black America and white America and Latino America and Asian America; there's the United States of America. The pundits like to slice-and-dice our country into Red States and Blue States; Red States for Republicans, Blue States for Democrats. But I've got news for them, too. We worship an awesome God in the Blue States, and we don't like federal agents poking around our libraries in the Red States. We coach Little League in the Blue States and have gay friends in the Red States. There are patriots who opposed the war in Iraq and patriots who supported it. We are one people, all of us pledging allegiance to the stars and stripes, all of us defending the United States of America.

In the end, that's what this election is about. Do we participate in a politics of cynicism or a politics of hope? John Kerry calls on us to hope. John Edwards calls on us to hope. I'm not talking about blind optimism here—the almost willful ignorance that thinks unemployment will go away if we just don't talk about it, or the health care crisis will solve itself if we just ignore it. No, I'm talking about something more substantial. It's the hope of slaves sitting around a fire singing freedom songs; the hope of immigrants setting out for distant shores; the hope of a young naval lieutenant bravely patrolling the Mekong Delta; the hope of a millworker's son who dares to defy the odds; the hope of a skinny kid with a funny name who believes that America has a place for him, too. The audacity of hope!

In the end, that is God's greatest gift to us, the bedrock of this nation; the belief in things not seen; the belief that there are better days ahead. I believe we can give our middle class relief and provide working families with a road to opportunity. I believe we can provide jobs to the jobless, homes to the homeless, and reclaim young people in cities across America from violence and despair. I believe that as we stand on the crossroads of history, we can make the right choices, and meet the challenges that face us. America!

Tonight, if you feel the same energy I do, the same urgency I do, the same passion I do, the same hopefulness I do—if we do what we must do, then I have no doubt that all across the country, from Florida to Oregon, from Washington to Maine, the people will rise up in November, and John Kerry will be sworn in as president, and John Edwards will be sworn in as vice president, and this country will reclaim its promise, and out of this long political darkness a brighter day will come. Thank you and God bless you.

U.S. Senator Barack Obama:

Speech to the

NationalPress Club

April 26, 2005

*T*hank you. It's great to be here at the National Press Club—I want to thank the club as well as the FDR Institute for arranging this luncheon together. I'd also like to thank Anne Roosevelt and Jim Roosevelt, who inspire us all by carrying on the proud legacy of their grandfather.

By the time the Senate Finance Committee holds the first Senate hearing on the President's Social Security plan today, we'll have heard just about everything there is to be said about the issue. We've heard about privatization and benefit cuts, about massive new debt and huge new risks, and we've even been scared into thinking the system will go broke when our kids retire, even though we know there'll be enough money then to pay the vast majority of benefits.

I'm happy to address some of these issues in the Q and A after the speech. But aside from the usual back and forth of this debate, I can't help but think about the larger issue at stake here.

Think about the America that Franklin Roosevelt saw when he looked out the windows of the White House from his wheelchair—an America where too many were ill-fed, ill-clothed, ill-housed, and insecure. An America where more and more Americans were finding themselves on the losing end of a new economy, and where there was nothing available to cushion their fall.

Some thought that our country didn't have a responsibility to do anything about these problems, that people would be better off left to their own devices and the whims of the market. Others believed that American capitalism had failed and that it was time to try something else altogether.

But our President believed deeply in the American idea.

He understood that the freedom to pursue our own individual dreams is made possible by the promise that if fate causes us to stumble or fall, our larger American family will be there to lift us up. That if we're willing to share even a small amount of life's risks and rewards with each other, then we'll all have the chance to make the most of our God-given potential.

And because Franklin Roosevelt had the courage to act on this idea, individual Americans were able to get back on their feet and build a shared prosperity that is still the envy of the world.

The New Deal gave the laid-off worker a guarantee that he could count on unemployment insurance to put food on his family's table while he looked for a new job. It gave the young man who suffered a debilitating accident assurance that he could count on disability benefits to get him through the tough times. A widow might still raise her children without the indignity of charity. And Franklin Roosevelt's greatest legacy promised the couple who put in a lifetime of sacrifice and hard work that they could retire in comfort and dignity because of Social Security.

Today, we're told by those who want to privatize that promise how much things are different and times have changed since Roosevelt's day.

I couldn't agree more.

A child born in this new century is likely to start his life with both parents—or a single parent—working full-time jobs. They'll try their hardest to juggle work and family, but they'll end up needing child care to keep him safe, cared for, and educated early.

They'll want to give him the best education possible, but unless they live in a wealthy town with good public schools, they'll have to settle for less or find the money for private schools.

This student will study hard and dream of going to the best colleges in the country, but with tuition rising higher and faster than ever before, he may have to postpone those dreams or start life deeper in debt than any generation before him.

When he graduates from college, this young man will find a job market where middle-class manufacturing jobs with good benefits have long been replaced with low-wage, low-benefit service sector jobs and high-skill, high-wage jobs of the future.

To get those good jobs, he'll need the skills and knowledge to not only compete with other workers in America, but with highly skilled and highly knowledgeable workers all over the world who are being recruited by the same companies that once made their home in this country.

When he finally starts his job, he'll want health insurance, but rising costs mean that fewer employers can afford to provide that benefit, and when they do, fewer employees can afford the record premiums.

When he starts a family, he'll want to buy a house and a car and pay for child care and college for his own children, but as he watches the lucky few benefit from lucrative bonuses and tax shelters, he'll see his own tax burden rise and his own paycheck barely cover this month's bills.

And when he retires, he'll hope that he and his wife have saved enough, but if there wasn't enough to save, he'll hope that there will still be two Social Security checks that come to the house every month.

These are the challenges we face at the beginning of the 21st century. We shouldn't exaggerate; we aren't seeing the absolute deprivation of the Great Depression. But it cannot be denied that families face more risk and greater insecurity than we have known since FDR's time, even as those families have fewer resources available to help pull themselves through the tough spots. Whereas people were once able to count on their employer to provide health care, pensions, and a job that would last a lifetime, today's worker wonders if suffering a heart attack will cause his employer to drop his coverage, worries about how much he can contribute to his own pension fund, and fears the possibility that he might walk into work tomorrow and find his job outsourced.

Yet, just as the naysayers in Roosevelt's day told us that there was nothing we could do to help people help themselves, the people in power today are telling us that instead of sharing the risks of the new economy, we should shoulder them on our own.

In the end, this is what the debate over the future of Social Security is truly about.

After a lifetime of hard work and contribution to this country, do we tell our seniors that they're on their own, or that we're here for them to provide a basic standard of living? Is the dignity of life in their latter years their problem, or one we all share?

Since this is Washington, you won't hear them answer those questions directly when they talk about Social Security. Instead, they use the word "reform" when they mean "privatize," and they use "strengthen" when they really mean "dismantle." They tell us there's a crisis to get us all riled up so we'll sit down and listen to their plan to privatize.

But we know what the whole thing's really about.

It's not just about cutting guaranteed benefits by up to 50%—though it certainly does that.

It's not just about borrowing $5 trillion from countries like China and Japan to finance the plan—after all, we know how fiscal conservatives hate debt and deficit.

And it's not even about the ability private accounts to finance the gap in the system—because even the privatization advocates admit they don't.

What this whole thing is about, and why conservatives have been pushing it so hard for so long now, is summed up in one sentence in one White House memo that somehow made its way out of the White House:

"For the first time in six decades, the Social Security battle is one we can win—and in doing so, we can help transform the political and philosophical landscape of the country."

And there it is. Since Social Security was first signed into law almost seventy years ago, at a time when FDR's opponents were calling it a hoax that would never work and some likened it to communism, there has been movement after movement to get rid of the program for purely ideological reasons. Because some still believe that we can't solve the problems we face as one American community; they think this country works better when we're left to face fate by ourselves.

I understand this view. There's something bracing about the Social Darwinist idea, the idea that there isn't a problem that the unfettered free market can't solve. It requires no sacrifice on the part of those of us who have won life's lottery...and doesn't consider who our parents were, or the education we received, or the right breaks that came at the right time.

But I couldn't disagree more. If we privatize Social Security, what will we tell retirees whose investments in the stock market went badly? We're sorry? Keep working? You're on your own?

When people's expected benefits get cut and they have to choose between their groceries and their prescriptions, what will we say then? That's not our problem?

When our debt climbs so high that our children face sky-high taxes just as they're starting their first job, what will we tell them? Deal with it yourselves?

This isn't how America works. This isn't how we saved millions of seniors from a life of poverty seventy years ago. This isn't how we sent a greatest generation of veterans to college so they could build the greatest middle-class in history. And this isn't how we should face the challenges of this new century either.

And yet, this is the direction they're trying to take America on almost every issue. Instead of trying to contain the skyrocketing cost of health care and expand access to the uninsured, the idea behind the President's Health Savings Accounts are to leave the system alone and give you a few extra bucks to go find a plan you can afford on your own. You deal with double digit inflation by going to the doctor less. Instead of strengthening a pension system that provides defined benefits to employees who've worked a lifetime, we'll give you a tax break and hope that you invest well and save well in your own little account. And if none of this works—if you couldn't find affordable insurance and suffer an illness that leaves you thousands of dollars in debt—then you should no longer count on being able to start over by declaring bankruptcy because they've changed the law to put the burden of debt squarely on your shoulders.

Taking responsibility for oneself and showing individual initiative are American values we all share. Frankly, they're values we could stand to see more of in a culture where the buck is too often passed to the next guy. They are values we could use more of here in Washington too.

But the irony of this all-out assault against every existing form of social insurance is that these safety nets are exactly what encourage each of us to be risk-takers and entrepreneurs who are free to pursue our individual ambitions. We get into a car knowing that if someone rear-ends us, they will have insurance to pay for the repairs. We buy a house knowing that our investment is protected by homeowners insurance. We take a chance on start-ups and small businesses because we know that if they fail, there are protections available to cushion our fall. Corporations across America have limited liability for this very reason. Families should too—and that's why we need social insurance. This is how the market works.

This is how America works. And if we want it to keep working, we need to develop new ways for all of us to share the new risks of a 21st century economy, not destroy what we already have.

The genius of Roosevelt was putting into practice the idea that America doesn't have to be a place where our individual aspirations are at war with our common good; it's a place where one makes the other possible.

I think we will save Social Security from privatization this year. And in doing so, we will affirm our belief that we are all connected as one people—ready to share life's risks and rewards for the benefit of each and the good of all.

Let me close by suggesting that Democrats are absolutely united in the need to strengthen Social Security and make it solvent for future generations. We know that, and we want that. And I believe that both Democrats and Republicans can work together to do that. While we're at it, we can begin a debate about the real challenges America faces as the baby boomers begin to retire.

About getting a handle on the growing cost of health care and prescription drugs. About increasing individual and national savings. About strengthening our pension system for the 21st century.

These are important questions that require us to work together, not in a manufactured panic about a genuine but solvable problem, but with the spirit of pragmatism and innovation that will offer every American the secure retirement they have earned.

You know, there are times in the life of this nation where we are individual citizens going about our own business, enjoying the freedoms we've been blessed with.

And then there are times when we are one America, linked by the dignity of each and the destiny of all.

The debate over the future of Social Security must be one of these times.

The people I've met since starting my campaign tell me they don't want a big government that's running their lives, but they do want an active government that will give them the opportunity to make the most of their lives.

Starting with the child born today and the senior moving into the twilight of life, together we can provide that opportunity.

The day Franklin Roosevelt signed the Social Security Act of 1935 into law, he began by saying that "Today, a hope of many years' standing is in large part fulfilled."

It is now time to fulfill our hope for an America where we're in this together—for our seniors, for our children, and for every American in the years and generations yet to come.

Thank you.

U.S. Senator Barack Obama: "Securing Our Energy Future"

Washington, DC

September 15, 2005

*A*s the flood waters recede in New Orleans and the survivors of Katrina begin to rebuild their lives, one truth has become achingly clear over the past few weeks:

Our government wasn't ready to save its own citizens from a catastrophe of biblical proportions. It wasn't even close.

Despite years of planning, preparing, and warnings from countless scientists, experts, and government officials—that the levees would break, that our first responders didn't have the best tools for communication, that FEMA was under-funded and undervalued—despite all of this, Katrina caught the government off-guard, flat-footed, and dangerously disorganized.

The most tragic consequence of this slow response was the incalculable loss of human life.

But miles off the Gulf Coast, as the deadly storm first raged towards shore, another frightening consequence emerged from our government's failure to prepare.

In the moments before the hurricane hit, Gulf refineries that made up one-eighth of our country's total capacity were evacuated and shut down. 95% of oil production was immediately suspended in a region where we find over a quarter of America's oil. And gas prices that were already at record highs shot up even further all over the country—reaching $6 a gallon in some places. Today, they're hovering over $3—a price that experts say will remain for the rest of the year. And what we don't see on television is how in a few months, the price of home heating oil and natural gas will reach new heights as well.

It would be one thing if this storm struck at a time of stability. But over the last few years, limited supplies and an unprecedented growth in demand have sent the global oil market itself teetering towards the edge of disaster. With our own Energy Department telling us that U.S. demand for oil will jump 40% over the next twenty years and countries like China and India adding millions of cars to their roads, the price of oil is reaching levels we just can't handle anymore.

A few years ago, we paid just $25 for a barrel of oil. Today, we're paying around $63. Since this affects the price of everything from gas to airfare to groceries, analysts at Global Insight, an economic consulting firm, say that if we hit $100 a barrel, the U.S. economy could very well tumble into recession.

Which brings me to one of the central lessons of Katrina, one that goes far beyond the gas hikes and the price gouging we're facing today:

The days of running a 21st century economy on a 20th century fossil fuel are numbered—and we need to realize that before it's too late.

Our persistent dependence on oil is a danger our government has known about for years. And despite constant warnings by researchers and scientists, major corporations and our own government officials, it's a danger they have failed to prepare for, listen to, or seriously try to guard against.

It's a danger we can no longer afford to ignore. Katrina, after all, was a natural disaster that affected only our domestic oil supply. But just imagine the threat to our national security from a geopolitical disaster—a war or an embargo—that cut off our supply from the rest of the world, where we get most of our oil.

Right now, we depend on some of the most politically volatile countries in the Middle East and elsewhere to fuel our energy needs. It doesn't matter if they're budding democracies, despotic regimes with nuclear intentions, or havens for the madrassas that plant the seeds of terror in young minds—they get our money because we need their oil.

What's worse—it's oil that's not very well protected. Over the last few years, we know that terrorists have stepped up their attempts to launch attacks on the poorly defended oil tankers and pipelines of the Middle East. And a former CIA agent tells us that if a terrorist hijacked a plane in Kuwait and crashed it into an oil complex in Saudi Arabia, it could take enough oil off the market to cause more economic damage than a direct attack on the United States.

At that point, $6 a gallon would look like a steal.

Hopefully, this short-term, hurricane-induced oil crisis will subside. But the clear and present danger to our economy and our security from America's long-term dependency on oil will not subside—unless we act now. In fact, it will only get worse.

As usual, the American people are already way ahead of Washington. Whether it's Galesburg farmers growing the corn that can fuel our cars or the Chicago factory workers making the microchip that let's us plug them in, people across the country have been taking America's energy future into their own hands with the same sense of innovation and optimism that sent the Wright brothers into the sky, led Dr. Salk to a cure for polio, and fueled Henry Ford's confidence that his workers could afford the cars they made.

But for too long now, this can-do spirit has been stifled by a can't-do government that seems to think it has no role in solving great national challenges or rallying a country to a cause. One that's content with simply giving more tax breaks to energy industries without asking for anything in return. Content with sending $650 million a day to countries like Saudi Arabia to pay for our fuel. And content with energy legislation that takes on only the easiest parts of the problem.

Now, I voted for the last energy bill. Because it took some baby steps in the right direction. It invests in the renewable, homegrown biofuels that could turn out to be some of the most promising alternatives to oil. It contains some provisions that would help us use alternative energy sources, increase our refinery capacity, and invest in clean coal technology. And recently, the administration made some executive policy changes that make it more difficult to classify cars as "light trucks," which would increase the production of more fuel-efficient cars.

None of these provisions do any harm—and a few do some good. But the energy bill and the administration's reforms don't suffer from sins of commission. Instead, they suffer from sins of omission. The solutions are too timid—the reforms too small. A bill that reduces our dependency on foreign oil by just 3% when our demand is about to jump 40% is not a serious energy policy. We need to do more.

The truth is, an oil future is not a secure future for America. Indeed, the rest of the world is already moving away from oil, and the longer we wait, the more difficult and painful it will be for our companies and our workers to catch up. Countries like China and Japan are creating jobs and slowing oil consumption by churning out and buying millions of fuel-efficient cars. Brazil, a nation that once relied on foreign countries to import 80% of its crude oil, will now be entirely self-sufficient in a few years thanks to its investment in biofuels. By getting more ethanol on the market and equipping their cars with the flexible-fuel engines that allow them to run on this fuel, Brazil has succeeded secured its energy supply while still giving consumers a break at the pump.

So why can't we do this? Why can't this be one of the great American projects of the 21st century?

The answer is, it can. We can do this with technology we have on the shelves right now; we can do it by saving, not crippling, our ailing auto companies; and we can do it by using the kind of clean, renewable sources of energy that we can literally grow right here in America.

There's no silver bullet. A solution to our energy dilemma won't come overnight. But we don't have to accept the wait-and-see attitude anymore. It flies in the face of our history and our founding principles. Katrina has shown us what could happen if we don't move away from an oil economy, but it has also provided us with a moment to challenge that kind of a future. Now is the time to seize that moment.

In the short-term, this probably means that we'll need to build even more refinery capacity and create not just a Strategic Petroleum Reserve, but also a Strategic Gasoline Reserve so that we can deal with the type of shortages we saw from Katrina. It means that we'll need to invest more in the clean technology that will allow us to burn more coal, our country's most abundant fossil fuel. And it means that we should continue to encourage the use of renewable fuels—by insisting that they make up 20% of our energy use and making sure that every new car in America has a flexible-fuel engine by 2010.

But we need to take even greater steps than these short-term measures. We need solutions that strike at the very heart of our dependence on oil.

Right now, the largest consumers of oil in this country are the cars we drive. And right now, we also have the technology to build cars that travel much further on a gallon of gas. We already have thousands of gas-electric hybrid cars driving around that can get 50 miles per gallon. Soon, plug-in hybrids will be able to get 75 miles per gallon. And experts believe that if we pump biofuels like E85 into a plug-in hybrid car, we can actually get up to 500 miles per gallon of gasoline.

So the technology is on the shelf. It's ready and available for our car companies to use. If we made sure that all passenger vehicles built in the U.S. got 40 miles per gallon, we would save consumers up to $5,000 at the pump over the life of their cars.

If we do this alone, we could reduce our dependence on foreign oil by over 1 billion barrels a year by 2020.

For years, we've hesitated to raise fuel economy standards as a nation in part because of a very legitimate concern—the impact it would have on Detroit. The auto industry is right when they argue that transitioning to more hybrid and fuel-efficient cars would require massive investment at a time when they're struggling under the weight of rising health care costs, sagging profits, and stiff competition from Europe and Japan.

But it's precisely because of that competition that they don't have a choice. As the demand and waiting lists for hybrid cars skyrocket, demand for SUVs—American car companies' biggest source of profit—is expected to plummet. The market is telling the auto industry to move away from oil—but so far only foreign companies are listening.

China now has a higher fuel economy standard than we do, and it's got 200,000 hybrids on its roads. Japan's Toyota is doubling production of the popular Prius to sell 100,000 in the U.S. this year, and it's getting ready to open a brand new production plant in China.

These companies are running circles around their American counterparts. Ford is only making 20,000 Escape Hybrids this year, and GM's brand won't be on the market until 2007. This isn't just costing us energy efficiency—it's decimating American businesses and costing American workers their jobs.

There is now no doubt that fuel-efficient cars represent the future of the auto industry. These cars will be built and bought and mass quantities. The only question is where and by who?

If American car companies hope to be a part of that future, if they hope to compete—if they hope to survive—they must make the necessary adjustments so that they can start building these cars. And we must help them do it.

There are many ways to do this and many good conversations that already taking place. One option is to provide direct subsidies to the auto industries so that it can transition its production to more fuel-efficient vehicles. Others have suggested providing tax credits for consumers to buy these cars.

Today I'd like to give you another example of a deal that Washington could make with Detroit. We'd start by raising the fuel economy standards in this country by 3% a year over the next fifteen years. But to help our auto industry make the transition—to give them the competitive edge they need against their foreign counterparts—we'd pay for part of the biggest costs they face today: retiree health care. Right now, health care costs represent $1,500 of the price of every GM car that's made. By picking up part of the tab for the health care costs of their retirees, we'd be lifting a huge burden off the auto industry so that they'll invest in the technology that will finally reduce America's dependence on foreign oil.

These solutions—investing in more hybrids and renewable energy sources; raising CAFE standards and helping our auto industry transition to a fuel-efficient future—represent a road to energy independence that will require some tough decisions and difficult politics, but as we look toward the future, it's the road we must travel as a nation. We could open up every square inch of America to drilling and we still wouldn't even make a dent in our oil dependency. We could open up ANWR today, and at its peak, which would be more than a decade from now, it would give us enough oil to take care of our transportation needs for about a month. Clearly, this is not a solution.

At the dawn of the Internet Age, Andy Grove of Intel famously said that there are two kinds of businesses: those that use email and those that will.

Today, there are two kinds of car companies: those who make fuel-efficient cars and those that will. We can't follow the world anymore. We must lead. And if we don't act now, the economic and societal benefits that have always been the hallmark of American innovation will find a home somewhere else.

There are few issues in American politics that have such a far-reaching effect on almost every aspect of our well-being as a nation, yet remain so absent from public interest and action. But as we cut through all the talk and the politics in the energy debate, we can see what the debate is really about.

We see the family that thinks twice about what they'll spend at the grocery store this week, because they've been paying $40 to fill up the tank for the last month. We see the grandmother who isn't sure how she'll make her Social Security check cover January's heating bill. The autoworker who isn't sure what the future at Ford holds for him. And the mother who sees turmoil in the Middle East and worries that someday her son might have to fight to secure our oil supply.

Ultimately, we see a nation that cannot control its future as long as it cannot control the source of energy that keeps it running.

Recently, I returned from a trip to Ukraine, where I had the opportunity to meet the nation's third president, Viktor Yushchenko. Since the country first broke away from the Soviet Union more than a decade earlier, Ukraine has been trying to forge its own identity and assert its own independence from Russia. This culminated earlier this year in the Orange Revolution, a mass demonstration from thousands of protestors who stood by Yushchenko and his promise to move his country further from the sphere of Russian influence.

President Yushchenko finally won. But today, Ukraine remains almost entirely dependent on—guess who—Russia—for all it's oil and gas supplies. And it is widely expected that in anticipation of next year's parliamentary elections, Russia will triple the prices of both. Despite all the soaring rhetoric, the demonstrations and the courage, Ukraine still finds itself at the mercy of its former patron—a nation that can now influence every political and economic decision they make—all because of oil.

This will not be America's future—but this is the stranglehold that fossil fuels can have on a nation's freedom. Ukraine may have little choice in the matter. The most powerful and wealthy nation on earth, teeming with brilliant minds and cutting-edge technology, surely does. The genius of the American people has already shown us the path towards energy independence, now they're just waiting for their government to take them there. Let's finally get it done. Thank you.

U.S. Senator Barack Obama: Speech to the Council on Foreign Relations "Non-Proliferation and Russia: The Challenges Ahead"

Washington, DC

November 1, 2005

*G*ood morning. As some of you know, Senator Lugar and I recently traveled to Russia, Ukraine, and Azerbaijan to witness firsthand both the progress we're making in securing the world's most dangerous weapons, as well as the serious challenges that lie ahead.

Senator Obama at the podiumNow, few people understand these challenges better than the co-founder of the Cooperative Threat Reduction Program, Dick Lugar, and this is something that became particularly clear to me during one incident on the trip.

We were in Ukraine, visiting a pathogen laboratory in Kiev. This is a city of two and a half million, and in a non-descript building right in the middle of town stood this facility that once operated on the fringes of the Soviet biological weapons program.

We entered through no fences or discernible security, and once we did, we found ourselves in a building with open first-floor windows and padlocks that many of us would not use to secure our own luggage.

Our guide then brought us right up to what looked like a mini-refrigerator. Inside, staring right at us, were rows upon rows of test tubes. She picked them up, clanked them around, and we listened to the translator explain what she was saying. Some of the tubes, he said, were filled with anthrax. Others, the plague.

At this point I turned around and said "Hey, where's Lugar? Doesn't he want to see this?" I found him standing about fifteen feet away, all the way in the back of the room. He looked at me and said, "Been there, done that."

Of course, Dick has been there and he has done that, and thanks to the Cooperative Threat Reduction Programs he co-founded with Senator Sam Nunn, we've made amazing progress in finding, securing, and guarding some of the deadliest weapons that were left scattered throughout the former Soviet Union after the Cold War.

But this is one story that shows our job is far from finished at a time when demand for these weapons has never been greater.

Right now, rogue states and despotic regimes are looking to begin or accelerate their own nuclear programs. And as we speak, members of Al Qaeda and other terrorists organizations are aggressively pursuing weapons of mass destruction, which they would use without hesitation.

We've heard the horror stories—attempts by rogue states to recruit former Soviet weapons scientists; terrorists shopping for weapons grade materials on the black market. Some weapons experts believe that terrorists are likely to find enough fissile material to build a bomb in the next ten years—and we can imagine with horror what the world will be like if they succeed.

Today, experts tell us that we're in a race against time to prevent this scenario from unfolding. And that is why the nuclear, chemical, and biological weapons within the borders of the former Soviet Union represent the greatest threat to the security of the United States—a threat we need to think seriously and intelligently about in the months to come.

Fortunately, the success of Cooperative Threat Reduction—especially in securing nuclear weapons—serves as a model of how we can do this. And so the question we need to be asking ourselves today is, what is the future of this program? With the situation in Russia and the rest of the former Soviet Union so drastically different than it was in 1991, or even in 1996 or 2001, what must we do to effectively confront this threat in the days and years to come?

The answers to these questions will require sustained involvement by the Executive Branch, Congress, non-governmental organizations, and the international community. Everyone has a role to play, and everyone must accelerate this involvement.

For my part, I would suggest three important elements that should be included in such a discussion.

First, the Nunn-Lugar program should be more engaged in containing proliferation threats from Soviet-supplied, civilian research reactors throughout Russia and the Independent States.

The Department of Energy and others have certainly made progress in converting civilian reactors to low-enriched uranium, taking back spent fuel, and closing unnecessary facilities.

Yet, a serious threat still remains. Many of these aging research facilities have the largest, least secure quantities of highly enriched uranium in the world—the quickest way to a nuclear weapon. For a scientist or other employee to simply walk out of the lab with enough material to construct a weapon of mass destruction is far too easy, and the consequences would be far too devastating. Not to mention the environmental and public health and safety catastrophe that could come from a failure to store and transport these materials safely and securely.

In a way that balances the needs of science and security, more needs to be done to bring these materials—as well as other sources that can be used to construct improvised nuclear weapons and radiological devices—under control and dramatically reduce the proliferation threat they pose.

In the years ahead, this should become an increasing priority for the Nunn-Lugar program, the Congress, and the Russians, who are already taking important steps to help implement these programs.

I want to turn to a second critical area: biological weapons threat reduction programs.

Throughout the Cold War, the Soviet Union was engaged in a massive undertaking in the field of germ warfare.

At its height in the late 1980's, this program stockpiled of some of the most dangerous agents known to man—plague, smallpox, and anthrax—to name just a few. As one book says, "disease by the ton was its industry."

Besides the devastation they can cause to a civilian population, biological agents can also be effective in asymmetrical warfare against U.S. troops. While they are often difficult to use, they are easy to transport, hard to detect, and, as we saw in Kiev, not always well secured.

Here in Washington, we saw what happened when just two letters filled with just a few grams of Anthrax were sent to the U.S. Senate. Five postal employees were killed and the Senate office buildings were closed for months.

This was two letters.

Fortunately, however, we've made some good progress on this front. For years, Nunn-Lugar programs have been effectively upgrading security at sites in six countries across the former Soviet Union. And the Kiev story is heading in the right direction—while we were in Ukraine, Dick, through his tireless and personal intervention, was able to achieve a breakthrough with that government, bringing that facility and others under the Cooperative Threat Reduction program.

But because of the size, secrecy, and scope of the Soviet biological weapons program, we are still dangerously behind in dealing with this proliferation threat. We need to be sure that Nunn-Lugar is increasingly focused on these very real non-proliferation and bioterrorism threats.

One of the most important steps is for Russia to permit the access and transparency necessary to deal with the threat.

Additional steps should also be taken to consolidate and secure dangerous pathogen collections, strengthen bio-reconnaissance networks to provide early warning of bio-attack and natural disease outbreaks, and have our experts work together to develop improved medical countermeasures. As the Avian Influenza outbreak demonstrates, even the zealous Russian border guard is helpless against the global sweep of biological threats.

My third recommendation—which I'll just touch briefly on and let Senator Lugar talk about in more detail—is that we need to start thinking creatively about some of the next-generation efforts on nuclear, biological, and chemical weapons.

On our trip, we saw two areas where this is possible: elimination of heavy conventional weapons, and interdiction efforts to help stop the flow of dangerous materials across borders.

In Donetsk, I stood among piles of conventional weapons that were slowly being dismantled. While the government of Ukraine is making progress here, the limited funding they have means that at the current pace, it will take sixty years to dismantle these weapons. But we've all seen how it could take far less time for these weapons to leak out and travel around the world, fueling insurgencies and violent conflicts from Africa to Afghanistan. By destroying these inventories, this is one place we could be making more of a difference.

One final point. For any of these efforts that I've mentioned to work as we move forward, we must also think critically and strategically about Washington's relationship with Moscow.

Right now, there are forces within the former Soviet Union and elsewhere that want these non-proliferation programs to stop. Our detention for three hours in Perm is a testament to these forces. Additionally, in the last few years, we've seen some disturbing trends from Russia itself—the deterioration of democracy and the rule of law, the abuses that have taken place in Chechnya, Russian meddling in the former Soviet Union—that raise serious questions about our relationship.

But when we think about the threat that these weapons pose to our global security, we cannot allow the U.S.-Russian relationship to deteriorate to the point where Russia does not think it's in their best interest to help us finish the job we started. We must safeguard these dangerous weapons, material, and expertise. .

One way we could strengthen this relationship is by thinking about the Russians as more of a partner and less of a subordinate in the Cooperative Threat Reduction effort.

This does not mean that we should ease up one bit on issues affecting our national security. Outstanding career officials who run the Nunn-Lugar program—people like Col. Jim Reid and Andy Weber who are here this morning—will be there every step of the way to ensure that U.S. interests are protected.

Time and time again on the trip, I saw their skill and experience when negotiating with the Russians. I also saw their ability to ensure that shortcomings were addressed and programs were implemented correctly.

But thinking of the Russians more as partners does mean being more thoughtful, respectful, and consistent about what we say and what we do. It means that the Russians can and should do more to support these programs. And it means more sustained engagement, including more senior-level visits to Nunn-Lugar program sites.

It's important for senior officials to go and visit these sites, to check their progress and shortcomings; to see what's working and what's not. But lately we haven't seen many of these visits. We need to see more.

We also need to ensure that the Cooperative Threat Reduction umbrella agreement, due to expire in 2006, is renewed in a timely manner.

And we need to work together to obtain a bilateral agreement on biological threat reduction.

There is no doubt that there is a tough road ahead. It will be difficult. And it will be dangerous.

But, when I think about what is at stake I am reminded by a quote from the late President Kennedy given in a speech at American University in 1963 about threats posed by the Soviet Union. "Let us not be blind to our differences—but let us also direct attention to our common interests and to the means by which those differences can be resolved...For in the final analysis, our most basic common link is that we all inhabit this small planet. We all breathe the same air. We all cherish our children's future. And we are all mortal."

Much of what President Kennedy described in 1963 remains true to this day—and we owe it to ourselves and our children to get it right.

Thank you.

U.S. Senator Barack Obama:
Speech to the
Chicago Council on Global Affairs
"A Way Forward in Iraq"

November 20, 2006

*T*hroughout American history, there have been moments that call on us to meet the challenges of an uncertain world, and pay whatever price is required to secure our freedom. They are the soul-trying times our forbearers spoke of, when the ease of complacency and self-interest must give way to the more difficult task of rendering judgment on what is best for the nation and for posterity, and then acting on that judgment—making the hard choices and sacrifices necessary to uphold our most deeply held values and ideals.

This was true for those who went to Lexington and Concord. It was true for those who lie buried at Gettysburg. It was true for those who built democracy's arsenal to vanquish fascism, and who then built a series of alliances and a world order that would ultimately defeat communism.

And this has been true for those of us who looked on the rubble and ashes of 9/11, and made a solemn pledge that such an atrocity would never again happen on United States soil; that we would do whatever it took to hunt down those responsible, and use every tool at our disposal—diplomatic, economic, and military—to root out both the agents of terrorism and the conditions that helped breed it.

In each case, what has been required to meet the challenges we face has been good judgment and clear vision from our leaders, and a fundamental seriousness and engagement on the part of the American people—a willingness on the part of each of us to look past what is petty and small and sensational, and look ahead to what is necessary and purposeful.

A few Tuesdays ago, the American people embraced this seriousness with regards to America's policy in Iraq. Americans were originally persuaded by the President to go to war in part because of the threat of weapons of mass destruction, and in part because they were told that it would help reduce the threat of international terrorism.

Neither turned out to be true. And now, after three long years of watching the same back and forth in Washington, the American people have sent a clear message that the days of using the war on terror as a political football are over. That policy-by-slogan will no longer pass as an acceptable form of debate in this country. "Mission Accomplished," "cut and run," "stay the course"—the American people have determined that all these phrases have become meaningless in the face of a conflict that grows more deadly and chaotic with each passing day—a conflict that has only increased the terrorist threat it was supposed to help contain.

2,867 Americans have now died in this war. Thousands more have suffered wounds that will last a lifetime. Iraq is descending into chaos based on ethnic divisions that were around long before American troops arrived. The conflict has left us distracted from containing the world's growing threats—in North Korea, in Iran, and in Afghanistan. And a report by our own intelligence agencies has concluded that al Qaeda is successfully using the war in Iraq to recruit a new generation of terrorists for its war on America.

These are serious times for our country, and with their votes two weeks ago, Americans demanded a feasible strategy with defined goals in Iraq—a strategy no longer driven by ideology and politics, but one that is based on a realistic assessment of the sobering facts on the ground and our interests in the region.

This kind of realism has been missing since the very conception of this war, and it is what led me to publicly oppose it in 2002. The notion that Iraq would quickly and easily become a bulwark of flourishing democracy in the Middle East was not a plan for victory, but an ideological fantasy. I said then and believe now that Saddam Hussein was a ruthless dictator who craved weapons of mass destruction but posed no imminent threat to the United States; that a war in Iraq would harm, not help, our efforts to defeat al Qaeda and finish the job in Afghanistan; and that an invasion would require an occupation of undetermined length, at undetermined cost, with undetermined consequences.

Month after month, and then year after year, I've watched with a heavy heart as my deepest suspicions about this war's conception have been confirmed and exacerbated in its disastrous implementation. No matter how bad it gets, we are told to wait, and not ask questions. We have been assured that the insurgency is in its last throes. We have been told that progress is just around the corner, and that when the Iraqis stand up, we will be able to stand down. Last week, without a trace of irony, the President even chose Vietnam as the backdrop for remarks counseling "patience" with his policies in Iraq.

When I came here and gave a speech on this war a year ago, I suggested that we begin to move towards a phased redeployment of American troops from Iraqi soil. At that point, seventy-five U.S. Senators, Republican and Democrat, including myself, had also voted in favor of a resolution demanding that 2006 be a year of significant transition in Iraq.

What we have seen instead is a year of significant deterioration. A year in which well-respected Republicans like John Warner, former Administration officials like Colin Powell, generals who have served in Iraq, and intelligence experts have all said that what we are doing is not working. A year that is ending with an attempt by the bipartisan Iraq Study Group to determine what can be done about a country that is quickly spiraling out of control.

According to our own Pentagon, the situation on the ground is now pointing towards chaos. Sectarian violence has reached an all-time high, and 365,000 Iraqis have fled their homes since the bombing of a Shia mosque in Samarra last February. 300,000 Iraqi security forces have supposedly been recruited and trained over the last two years, and yet American troop levels have not been reduced by a single soldier. The addition of 4,000 American troops in Baghdad has not succeeded in securing that increasingly perilous city. And polls show that almost two-thirds of all Iraqis now sympathize with attacks on American soldiers.

Prime Minister Maliki is not making our job easier. In just the past three weeks, he has—and I'm quoting from a New York Times article here—"rejected the notion of an American 'timeline' for action on urgent Iraqi political issues; ordered American commanders to lift checkpoints they had set up around the Shiite district of Sadr City to hunt for a kidnapped American soldier and a fugitive Shiite death squad leader; and blamed the Americans for the deteriorating security situation in Iraq."

This is now the reality of Iraq.

Now, I am hopeful that the Iraq Study Group emerges next month with a series of proposals around which we can begin to build a bipartisan consensus. I am committed to working with this White House and any of my colleagues in the months to come to craft such a consensus. And I believe that it remains possible to salvage an acceptable outcome to this long and misguided war.

But it will not be easy. For the fact is that there are no good options left in this war. There are no options that do not carry significant risks. And so the question is not whether there is some magic formula for success, or guarantee against failure, in Iraq. Rather, the question is what strategies, imperfect though they may be, are most likely to achieve the best outcome in Iraq, one that will ultimately put us on a more effective course to deal with international terrorism, nuclear proliferation, and other critical threats to our security.

What is absolutely clear is that it is not enough for the President to respond to Iraq's reality by saying that he is "open to" or "interested in" new ideas while acting as if all that's required is doing more of the same. It is not enough for him to simply lay out benchmarks for progress with no consequences attached for failing to meet them. And it is not enough for the President to tell us that victory in this war is simply a matter of American resolve. The American people have been extraordinarily resolved. They have seen their sons and daughters killed or wounded in the streets of Fallujah. They have spent hundreds of billions of their hard-earned dollars on this effort—money that could have been devoted to strengthening our homeland security and our competitive standing as a nation. No, it has not been a failure of resolve that has led us to this chaos, but a failure of strategy—and that strategy must change.

It may be politically advantageous for the President to simply define victory as staying and defeat as leaving, but it prevents a serious conversation about the realistic objectives we can still achieve in Iraq. Dreams of democracy and hopes for a perfect government are now just that—dreams and hopes. We must instead turn our focus to those concrete objectives that are possible to attain—namely, preventing Iraq from becoming what Afghanistan once was, maintaining our influence in the Middle East, and forging a political settlement to stop the sectarian violence so that our troops can come home.

There is no reason to believe that more of the same will achieve these objectives in Iraq. And, while some have proposed escalating this war by adding thousands of more troops, there is little reason to believe that this will achieve these results either. It's not clear that these troop levels are sustainable for a significant period of time, and according to our commanders on the ground, adding American forces will only relieve the Iraqis from doing more on their own. Moreover, without a coherent strategy or better cooperation from the Iraqis, we would only be putting more of our soldiers in the crossfire of a civil war.

Let me underscore this point. The American soldiers I met when I traveled to Iraq this year were performing their duties with bravery, with brilliance, and without question. They are doing so today. They have battled insurgents, secured cities, and maintained some semblance of order in Iraq. But even as they have carried out their responsibilities with excellence and valor, they have also told me that there is no military solution to this war. Our troops can help suppress the violence, but they cannot solve its root causes. And all the troops in the world won't be able to force Shia, Sunni, and Kurd to sit down at a table, resolve their differences, and forge a lasting peace.

I have long said that the only solution in Iraq is a political one. To reach such a solution, we must communicate clearly and effectively to the factions in Iraq that the days of asking, urging, and waiting for them to take control of their own country are coming to an end. No more coddling, no more equivocation. Our best hope for success is to use the tools we have—military, financial, diplomatic—to pressure the Iraqi leadership to finally come to a political agreement between the warring factions that can create some sense of stability in the country and bring this conflict under control.

The first part of this strategy begins by exerting the greatest leverage we have on the Iraqi government—a phased redeployment of U.S. troops from Iraq on a timetable that would begin in four to six months.

When I first advocated steps along these lines over a year ago, I had hoped that this phased redeployment could begin by the end of 2006. Such a timetable may now need to begin in 2007, but begin it must. For only through this phased redeployment can we send a clear message to the Iraqi factions that the U.S. is not going to hold together this country indefinitely—that it will be up to them to form a viable government that can effectively run and secure Iraq.

Let me be more specific. The President should announce to the Iraqi people that our policy will include a gradual and substantial reduction in U.S. forces. He should then work with our military commanders to map out the best plan for such a redeployment and determine precise levels and dates. When possible, this should be done in consultation with the Iraqi government—but it should not depend on Iraqi approval.

I am not suggesting that this timetable be overly-rigid. We cannot compromise the safety of our troops, and we should be willing to adjust to realities on the ground. The redeployment could be temporarily suspended if the parties in Iraq reach an effective political arrangement that stabilizes the situation and they offer us a clear and compelling rationale for maintaining certain troop levels. Moreover, it could be suspended if at any point U.S. commanders believe that a further reduction would put American troops in danger.

Drawing down our troops in Iraq will allow us to redeploy additional troops to Northern Iraq and elsewhere in the region as an over-the-horizon force. This force could help prevent the conflict in Iraq from becoming a wider war, consolidate gains in Northern Iraq, reassure allies in the Gulf, allow our troops to strike directly at al Qaeda wherever it may exist, and demonstrate to international terrorist organizations that they have not driven us from the region.

Perhaps most importantly, some of these troops could be redeployed to Afghanistan, where our lack of focus and commitment of resources has led to an increasing deterioration of the security situation there. The President's decision to go to war in Iraq has had disastrous consequences for Afghanistan—we have seen a fierce Taliban offensive, a spike in terrorist attacks, and a narcotrafficking problem spiral out of control. Instead of consolidating the gains made by the Karzai government, we are backsliding towards chaos. By redeploying from Iraq to Afghanistan, we will answer NATO's call for more troops and provide a much-needed boost to this critical fight against terrorism.

As a phased redeployment is executed, the majority of the U.S. troops remaining in Iraq should be dedicated to the critical, but less visible roles, of protecting logistics supply points, critical infrastructure, and American enclaves like the Green Zone, as well as acting as a rapid reaction force to respond to emergencies and go after terrorists.

In such a scenario, it is conceivable that a significantly reduced U.S. force might remain in Iraq for a more extended period of time. But only if U.S. commanders think such a force would be effective; if there is substantial movement towards a political solution among Iraqi factions; if the Iraqi government showed a serious commitment to disbanding the militias; and if the Iraqi government asked us—in a public and unambiguous way—for such continued support. We would make clear in such a scenario that the United States would not be maintaining permanent military bases in Iraq, but would do what was necessary to help prevent a total collapse of the Iraqi state and further polarization of Iraqi society. Such a reduced but active presence will also send a clear message to hostile countries like Iran and Syria that we intend to remain a key player in this region.

The second part of our strategy should be to couple this phased redeployment with a more effective plan that puts the Iraqi security forces in the lead, intensifies and focuses our efforts to train those forces, and expands the numbers of our personnel—especially special forces—who are deployed with Iraqi units as advisers.

An increase in the quality and quantity of U.S. personnel in training and advisory roles can guard against militia infiltration of Iraqi units; develop the trust and goodwill of Iraqi soldiers and the local populace; and lead to better intelligence while undercutting grassroots support for the insurgents.

Let me emphasize one vital point—any U.S. strategy must address the problem of sectarian militias in Iraq. In the absence of a genuine commitment on the part of all of the factions in Iraq to deal with this issue, it is doubtful that a unified Iraqi government can function for long, and it is doubtful that U.S. forces, no matter how large, can prevent an escalation of widespread sectarian killing.

Of course, in order to convince the various factions to embark on the admittedly difficult task of disarming their militias, the Iraqi government must also make headway on reforming the institutions that support the military and the police. We can teach the soldiers to fight and police to patrol, but if the Iraqi government will not properly feed, adequately pay, or provide them with the equipment they need, they will continue to desert in large numbers, or maintain fealty only to their religious group rather than the national government. The security forces have to be far more inclusive—standing up an army composed mainly of Shiites and Kurds will only cause the Sunnis to feel more threatened and fight even harder.

The third part of our strategy should be to link continued economic aid in Iraq with the existence of tangible progress toward a political settlement.

So far, Congress has given the Administration unprecedented flexibility in determining how to spend more than $20 billion dollars in Iraq. But instead of effectively targeting this aid, we have seen some of the largest waste, fraud, and abuse of foreign aid in American history. Today, the Iraqi landscape is littered with ill-conceived, half-finished projects that have done almost nothing to help the Iraqi people or stabilize the country.

This must end in the next session of Congress, when we reassert our authority to oversee the management of this war. This means no more bloated no-bid contracts that cost the taxpayers millions in overhead and administrative expenses.

We need to continue to provide some basic reconstruction funding that will be used to put Iraqis to work and help our troops stabilize key areas. But we need to also move towards more condition-based aid packages where economic assistance is contingent upon the ability of Iraqis to make measurable progress on reducing sectarian violence and forging a lasting political settlement.

Finally, we have to realize that the entire Middle East has an enormous stake in the outcome of Iraq, and we must engage neighboring countries in finding a solution.

This includes opening dialogue with both Syria and Iran, an idea supported by both James Baker and Robert Gates. We know these countries want us to fail, and we should remain steadfast in our opposition to their support of terrorism and Iran's nuclear ambitions. But neither Iran nor Syria want to see a security vacuum in Iraq filled with chaos, terrorism, refugees, and violence, as it could have a destabilizing effect throughout the entire region—and within their own countries.

And so I firmly believe that we should convene a regional conference with the Iraqis, Saudis, Iranians, Syrians, the Turks, Jordanians, the British and others. The goal of this conference should be to get foreign fighters out of Iraq, prevent a further descent into civil war, and push the various Iraqi factions towards a political solution.

Make no mistake—if the Iranians and Syrians think they can use Iraq as another Afghanistan or a staging area from which to attack Israel or other countries, they are badly mistaken. It is in our national interest to prevent this from happening. We should also make it clear that, even after we begin to drawdown forces, we will still work with our allies in the region to combat international terrorism and prevent the spread of weapons of mass destruction. It is simply not productive for us not to engage in discussions with Iran and Syria on an issue of such fundamental importance to all of us.

This brings me to a set of broader points. As we change strategy in Iraq, we should also think about what Iraq has taught us about America's strategy in the wider struggle against rogue threats and international terrorism.

Many who supported the original decision to go to war in Iraq have argued that it has been a failure of implementation. But I have long believed it has also been a failure of conception—that the rationale behind the war itself was misguided. And so going forward, I believe there are strategic lessons to be learned from this as we continue to confront the new threats of this new century.

The first is that we should be more modest in our belief that we can impose democracy on a country through military force. In the past, it has been movements for freedom from within tyrannical regimes that have led to flourishing democracies; movements that continue today. This doesn't mean abandoning our values and ideals; wherever we can, it's in our interest to help foster democracy through the diplomatic and economic resources at our disposal. But even as we provide such help, we should be clear that the institutions of democracy—free markets, a free press, a strong civil society—cannot be built overnight, and they cannot be built at the end of a barrel of a gun. And so we must realize that the freedoms FDR once spoke of—especially freedom from want and freedom from fear—do not just come from deposing a tyrant and handing out ballots; they are only realized once the personal and material security of a people is ensured as well.

The second lesson is that in any conflict, it is not enough to simply plan for war; you must also plan for success. Much has been written about how the military invasion of Iraq was planned without any thought to what political situation we would find after Baghdad fell. Such lack of foresight is simply inexcusable. If we commit our troops anywhere in the world, it is our solemn responsibility to define their mission and formulate a viable plan to fulfill that mission and bring our troops home.

The final lesson is that in an interconnected world, the defeat of international terrorism—and most importantly, the prevention of these terrorist organizations from obtaining weapons of mass destruction—will require the cooperation of many nations. We must always reserve the right to strike unilaterally at terrorists wherever they may exist. But we should know that our success in doing so is enhanced by engaging our allies so that we receive the crucial diplomatic, military, intelligence, and financial support that can lighten our load and add legitimacy to our actions. This means talking to our friends and, at times, even our enemies.

We need to keep these lessons in mind as we think about the broader threats America now faces—threats we haven't paid nearly enough attention to because we have been distracted in Iraq.

The National Intelligence Estimate, which details how we're creating more terrorists in Iraq than we're defeating, is the most obvious example of how the war is hurting our efforts in the larger battle against terrorism. But there are many others.

The overwhelming presence of our troops, our intelligence, and our resources in Iraq has stretched our military to the breaking point and distracted us from the growing threats of a dangerous world. The Chairman of the Joint Chiefs recently said that if a conflict arose in North Korea, we'd have to largely rely on the Navy and Air Force to take care of it, since the Army and Marines are engaged elsewhere. In my travels to Africa, I have seen weak governments and broken societies that can be exploited by al Qaeda. And on a trip to the former Soviet Union, I have seen the biological and nuclear weapons terrorists could easily steal while the world looks the other way.

There is one other place where our mistakes in Iraq have cost us dearly—and that is the loss of our government's credibility with the American people. According to a Pew survey, 42% of Americans now agree with the statement that the U.S. should "mind its own business internationally and let other countries get along the best they can on their own."

We cannot afford to be a country of isolationists right now. 9/11 showed us that try as we might to ignore the rest of the world, our enemies will no longer ignore us. And so we need to maintain a strong foreign policy, relentless in pursuing our enemies and hopeful in promoting our values around the world.

But to guard against isolationist sentiments in this country, we must change conditions in Iraq and the policy that has characterized our time there—a policy based on blind hope and ideology instead of fact and reality.

Americans called for this more serious policy a few Tuesdays ago. It's time that we listen to their concerns and win back their trust. I spoke here a year ago and delivered a message about Iraq that was similar to the one I did today. I refuse to accept the possibility that I will have to come back a year from now and say the same thing.

There have been too many speeches. There have been too many excuses. There have been too many flag-draped coffins, and there have been too many heartbroken families.

The time for waiting in Iraq is over. It is time to change our policy. It is time to give Iraqis their country back. And it is time to refocus America's efforts on the wider struggle yet to be won.

Thank you.

U.S. Senator Barack Obama: Announcement That He Will Run for the Office of the President of the United States

Springfield, IL

February 10, 2007

*L*et me begin by saying thanks to all you who've traveled, from far and wide, to brave the cold today.

We all made this journey for a reason. It's humbling, but in my heart I know you didn't come here just for me, you came here because you believe in what this country can be. In the face of war, you believe there can be peace. In the face of despair, you believe there can be hope. In the face of a politics that's shut you out, that's told you to settle, that's divided us for too long, you believe we can be one people, reaching for what's possible, building that more perfect union.

That's the journey we're on today. But let me tell you how I came to be here. As most of you know, I am not a native of this great state. I moved to Illinois over two decades ago. I was a young man then, just a year out of college; I knew no one in Chicago, was without money or family connections. But a group of churches had offered me a job as a community organizer for $13,000 a year. And I accepted the job, sight unseen, motivated then by a single, simple, powerful idea—that I might play a small part in building a better America.

My work took me to some of Chicago's poorest neighborhoods. I joined with pastors and lay-people to deal with communities that had been ravaged by plant closings. I saw that the problems people faced weren't simply local in nature—that the decision to close a steel mill was made by distant executives; that the lack of textbooks and computers in schools could be traced to the skewed priorities of politicians a thousand miles away; and that when a child turns to violence, there's a hole in his heart no government alone can fill.

It was in these neighborhoods that I received the best education I ever had, and where I learned the true meaning of my Christian faith.

After three years of this work, I went to law school, because I wanted to understand how the law should work for those in need. I became a civil rights lawyer, and taught constitutional law, and after a time, I came to understand that our cherished rights of liberty and equality depend on the active participation of an awakened electorate. It was with these ideas in mind that I arrived in this capital city as a state Senator.

It was here, in Springfield, where I saw all that is America converge— farmers and teachers, businessmen and laborers, all of them with a story to tell, all of them seeking a seat at the table, all of them clamoring to be heard. I made lasting friendships here—friends that I see in the audience today.

It was here we learned to disagree without being disagreeable—that it's possible to compromise so long as you know those principles that can never be compromised; and that so long as we're willing to listen to each other, we can assume the best in people instead of the worst.

That's why we were able to reform a death penalty system that was broken. That's why we were able to give health insurance to children in need. That's why we made the tax system more fair and just for working families, and that's why we passed ethics reforms that the cynics said could never, ever be passed.

It was here, in Springfield, where North, South, East and West come together that I was reminded of the essential decency of the American people—where I came to believe that through this decency, we can build a more hopeful America.

And that is why, in the shadow of the Old State Capitol, where Lincoln once called on a divided house to stand together, where common hopes and common dreams still, I stand before you today to announce my candidacy for President of the United States.

I recognize there is a certain presumptuousness—a certain audacity— to this announcement. I know I haven't spent a lot of time learning the ways of Washington. But I've been there long enough to know that the ways of Washington must change.

The genius of our founders is that they designed a system of government that can be changed. And we should take heart, because we've changed this country before. In the face of tyranny, a band of patriots brought an Empire to its knees. In the face of secession, we unified a nation and set the captives free. In the face of Depression, we put people back to work and lifted millions out of poverty. We welcomed immigrants to our shores, we opened railroads to the west, we landed a man on the moon, and we heard a King's call to let justice roll down like water, and righteousness like a mighty stream.

Each and every time, a new generation has risen up and done what's needed to be done. Today we are called once more—and it is time for our generation to answer that call.

For that is our unyielding faith—that in the face of impossible odds, people who love their country can change it.

That's what Abraham Lincoln understood. He had his doubts. He had his defeats. He had his setbacks. But through his will and his words, he moved a nation and helped free a people. It is because of the millions who rallied to his cause that we are no longer divided, North and South, slave and free. It is because men and women of every race, from every walk of life, continued to march for freedom long after Lincoln was laid to rest, that today we have the chance to face the challenges of this millennium together, as one people—as Americans.

All of us know what those challenges are today—a war with no end, a dependence on oil that threatens our future, schools where too many children aren't learning, and families struggling paycheck to paycheck despite working as hard as they can. We know the challenges. We've heard them. We've talked about them for years.

What's stopped us from meeting these challenges is not the absence of sound policies and sensible plans. What's stopped us is the failure of leadership, the smallness of our politics—the ease with which we're distracted by the petty and trivial, our chronic avoidance of tough decisions, our preference for scoring cheap political points instead of rolling up our sleeves and building a working consensus to tackle big problems.

For the last six years we've been told that our mounting debts don't matter, we've been told that the anxiety Americans feel about rising health care costs and stagnant wages are an illusion, we've been told that climate change is a hoax, and that tough talk and an ill-conceived war can replace diplomacy, and strategy, and foresight. And when all else fails, when Katrina happens, or the death toll in Iraq mounts, we've been told that our crises are somebody else's fault. We're distracted from our real failures, and told to blame the other party, or gay people, or immigrants.

And as people have looked away in disillusionment and frustration, we know what's filled the void. The cynics, and the lobbyists, and the special interests who've turned our government into a game only they can afford to play. They write the checks and you get stuck with the bills, they get the access while you get to write a letter, they think they own this government, but we're here today to take it back. The time for that politics is over. It's time to turn the page.

We've made some progress already. I was proud to help lead the fight in Congress that led to the most sweeping ethics reform since Watergate.

But Washington has a long way to go. And it won't be easy. That's why we'll have to set priorities. We'll have to make hard choices. And although government will play a crucial role in bringing about the changes we need, more money and programs alone will not get us where we need to go. Each of us, in our own lives, will have to accept responsibility—for instilling an ethic of achievement in our children, for adapting to a more competitive economy, for strengthening our communities, and sharing some measure of sacrifice. So let us begin. Let us begin this hard work together. Let us transform this nation.

Let us be the generation that reshapes our economy to compete in the digital age. Let's set high standards for our schools and give them the resources they need to succeed. Let's recruit a new army of teachers, and give them better pay and more support in exchange for more accountability. Let's make college more affordable, and let's invest in scientific research, and let's lay down broadband lines through the heart of inner cities and rural towns all across America.

And as our economy changes, let's be the generation that ensures our nation's workers are sharing in our prosperity. Let's protect the hard-earned benefits their companies have promised. Let's make it possible for hardworking Americans to save for retirement. And let's allow our unions and their organizers to lift up this country's middle-class again.

Let's be the generation that ends poverty in America. Every single person willing to work should be able to get job training that leads to a job, and earn a living wage that can pay the bills, and afford child care so their kids have a safe place to go when they work. Let's do this.

Let's be the generation that finally tackles our health care crisis. We can control costs by focusing on prevention, by providing better treatment to the chronically ill, and using technology to cut the bureaucracy. Let's be the generation that says right here, right now, that we will have universal health care in America by the end of the next president's first term.

Let's be the generation that finally frees America from the tyranny of oil. We can harness homegrown, alternative fuels like ethanol and spur the production of more fuel-efficient cars. We can set up a system for capping greenhouse gases. We can turn this crisis of global warming into a moment of opportunity for innovation, and job creation, and an incentive for businesses that will serve as a model for the world. Let's be the generation that makes future generations proud of what we did here.

Most of all, let's be the generation that never forgets what happened on that September day and confront the terrorists with everything we've got. Politics doesn't have to divide us on this anymore—we can work together to keep our country safe. I've worked with Republican Senator Dick Lugar to pass a law that will secure and destroy some of the world's deadliest, unguarded weapons. We can work together to track terrorists down with a stronger military, we can tighten the net around their finances, and we can improve our intelligence capabilities. But let us also understand that ultimate victory against our enemies will come only by rebuilding our alliances and exporting those ideals that bring hope and opportunity to millions around the globe.

But all of this cannot come to pass until we bring an end to this war in Iraq. Most of you know I opposed this war from the start. I thought it was a tragic mistake. Today we grieve for the families who have lost loved ones, the hearts that have been broken, and the young lives that could have been. America, it's time to start bringing our troops home. It's time to admit that no amount of American lives can resolve the political disagreement that lies at the heart of someone else's civil war. That's why I have a plan that will bring our combat troops home by March of 2008. Letting the Iraqis know that we will not be there forever is our last, best hope to pressure the Sunni and Shia to come to the table and find peace.

Finally, there is one other thing that is not too late to get right about this war—and that is the homecoming of the men and women—our veterans—who have sacrificed the most. Let us honor their valor by providing the care they need and rebuilding the military they love. Let us be the generation that begins this work.

I know there are those who don't believe we can do all these things. I understand the skepticism. After all, every four years, candidates from both parties make similar promises, and I expect this year will be no different. All of us running for president will travel around the country offering ten-point plans and making grand speeches; all of us will trumpet those qualities we believe make us uniquely qualified to lead the country. But too many times, after the election is over, and the confetti is swept away, all those promises fade from memory, and the lobbyists and the special interests move in, and people turn away, disappointed as before, left to struggle on their own.

That is why this campaign can't only be about me. It must be about us—it must be about what we can do together. This campaign must be the occasion, the vehicle, of your hopes, and your dreams. It will take your time, your energy, and your advice—to push us forward when we're doing right, and to let us know when we're not. This campaign has to be about reclaiming the meaning of citizenship, restoring our sense of common purpose, and realizing that few obstacles can withstand the power of millions of voices calling for change.

By ourselves, this change will not happen. Divided, we are bound to fail.

But the life of a tall, gangly, self-made Springfield lawyer tells us that a different future is possible.

He tells us that there is power in words.

He tells us that there is power in conviction.

That beneath all the differences of race and region, faith and station, we are one people.

He tells us that there is power in hope.

As Lincoln organized the forces arrayed against slavery, he was heard to say: "Of strange, discordant, and even hostile elements, we gathered from the four winds, and formed and fought to battle through."

That is our purpose here today.

That's why I'm in this race.

Not just to hold an office, but to gather with you to transform a nation.

I want to win that next battle—for justice and opportunity.

I want to win that next battle—for better schools, and better jobs, and health care for all.

I want us to take up the unfinished business of perfecting our union, and building a better America.

And if you will join me in this improbable quest, if you feel destiny calling, and see as I see, a future of endless possibility stretching before us; if you sense, as I sense, that the time is now to shake off our slumber, and slough off our fear, and make good on the debt we owe past and future generations, then I'm ready to take up the cause, and march with you, and work with you. Together, starting today, let us finish the work that needs to be done, and usher in a new birth of freedom on this Earth.

U.S. Senator Barack Obama: "A Politics of Conscience"

Hartford, CT

June 23, 2007

*I*t's great to be here. I've been speaking to a lot of churches recently, so it's nice to be speaking to one that's so familiar. I understand you switched venues at considerable expense and inconvenience because of unfair labor practices at the place you were going to be having this synod. Clearly, the past 50 years have not weakened your resolve as faithful witnesses of the gospel. And I'm glad to see that.

It's been several months now since I announced I was running for president. In that time, I've had the chance to talk with Americans all across this country. And I've found that no matter where I am, or who I'm talking to, there's a common theme that emerges. It's that folks are hungry for change—they're hungry for something new. They're ready to turn the page on the old politics and the old policies—whether it's the war in Iraq or the health care crisis we're in, or a school system that's leaving too many kids behind despite the slogans.

But I also get the sense that there's a hunger that's deeper than that—a hunger that goes beyond any single cause or issue. It seems to me that each day, thousands of Americans are going about their lives—dropping the kids off at school, driving to work, shopping at the mall, trying to stay on their diets, trying to kick a cigarette habit—and they're coming to the realization that something is missing. They're deciding that their work, their possessions, their diversions, their sheer busyness, is not enough.

They want a sense of purpose, a narrative arc to their lives. They're looking to relieve a chronic loneliness. And so they need an assurance that somebody out there cares about them, is listening to them—that they are not just destined to travel down that long road toward nothingness.

And this restlessness—this search for meaning—is familiar to me. I was not raised in a particularly religious household. My father, who I didn't know, returned to Kenya when I was just two. He was nominally a Muslim since there were a number of Muslims in the village where he was born.

But by the time he was a young adult, he was an atheist. My mother, whose parents were non-practicing Baptists and Methodists, was one of the most spiritual souls I ever knew. She had this enormous capacity for wonder, and lived by the Golden Rule. But she had a healthy skepticism of religion as an institution. And as a consequence, so did I.

It wasn't until after college, when I went to Chicago to work as a community organizer for a group of Christian churches, that I confronted my own spiritual dilemma. In a sense, what brought me to Chicago in the first place was a hunger for some sort of meaning in my life. I wanted to be part of something larger. I'd been inspired by the civil rights movement—by all the clear-eyed, straight-backed, courageous young people who'd boarded buses and traveled down South to march and sit at lunch counters, and lay down their lives in some cases for freedom. I was too young to be involved in that movement, but I felt I could play a small part in the continuing battle for justice by helping rebuild some of Chicago's poorest neighborhoods.

So it's 1985, and I'm in Chicago, and I'm working with these churches, and with lots of laypeople who are much older than I am. And I found that I recognized in these folks a part of myself. I learned that everyone's got a sacred story when you take the time to listen. And I think they recognized a part of themselves in me too. They saw that I knew the Scriptures and that many of the values I held and that propelled me in my work were values they shared. But I think they also sensed that a part of me remained removed and detached—that I was an observer in their midst.

And slowly, I came to realize that something was missing as well—that without an anchor for my beliefs, without a commitment to a particular community of faith, at some level I would always remain apart, and alone.

And it's around this time that some pastors I was working with came up to me and asked if I was a member of a church. "If you're organizing churches," they said, "it might be helpful if you went to church once in a while." And I thought, "Well, I guess that makes sense."

So one Sunday, I put on one of the few clean jackets I had, and went over to Trinity United Church of Christ on 95th Street on the South Side of Chicago. And I heard Reverend Jeremiah A. Wright deliver a sermon called "The Audacity of Hope." And during the course of that sermon, he introduced me to someone named Jesus Christ. I learned that my sins could be redeemed. I learned that those things I was too weak to accomplish myself, He would accomplish with me if I placed my trust in Him. And in time, I came to see faith as more than just a comfort to the weary or a hedge against death, but rather as an active, palpable agent in the world and in my own life.

It was because of these newfound understandings that I was finally able to walk down the aisle of Trinity one day and affirm my Christian faith. It came about as a choice, and not an epiphany. I didn't fall out in church, as folks sometimes do. The questions I had didn't magically disappear. The skeptical bent of my mind didn't suddenly vanish. But kneeling beneath that cross on the South Side, I felt I heard God's spirit beckoning me. I submitted myself to His will, and dedicated myself to discovering His truth and carrying out His works.

But my journey is part of a larger journey—one shared by all who've ever sought to apply the values of their faith to our society. It's a journey that takes us back to our nation's founding, when none other than a UCC church inspired the Boston Tea Party and helped bring an Empire to its knees. In the following century, men and women of faith waded into the battles over prison reform and temperance, public education and women's rights—and above all, abolition. And when the Civil War was fought and our country dedicated itself to a new birth of freedom, they took on the problems of an industrializing nation—fighting the crimes against society and the sins against God that they felt were being committed in our factories and in our slums.

And when these battles were overtaken by others and when the wars they opposed were waged and won, these faithful foot soldiers for justice kept marching. They stood on the Edmund Pettus Bridge, as the blows of billy clubs rained down. They held vigils across this country when four little girls were killed in the 16th Street Baptist Church. They cheered on the steps of the Lincoln Memorial when Dr. King delivered his prayer for our country. And in all these ways, they helped make this country more decent and more just.

So doing the Lord's work is a thread that's run through our politics since the very beginning. And it puts the lie to the notion that the separation of church and state in America means faith should have no role in public life. Imagine Lincoln's Second Inaugural without its reference to "the judgments of the Lord." Or King's "I Have a Dream" speech without its reference to "all of God's children." Or President Kennedy's Inaugural without the words, "here on Earth, God's work must truly be our own." At each of these junctures, by summoning a higher truth and embracing a universal faith, our leaders inspired ordinary people to achieve extraordinary things.

But somehow, somewhere along the way, faith stopped being used to bring us together and started being used to drive us apart. It got hijacked. Part of it's because of the so-called leaders of the Christian Right, who've been all too eager to exploit what divides us. At every opportunity, they've told evangelical Christians that Democrats disrespect their values and dislike their Church, while suggesting to the rest of the country that religious Americans care only about issues like abortion and gay marriage; school prayer and intelligent design. There was even a time when the Christian Coalition determined that its number one legislative priority was tax cuts for the rich. I don't know what Bible they're reading, but it doesn't jibe with my version.

But I'm hopeful because I think there's an awakening taking place in America. People are coming together around a simple truth—that we are all connected, that I am my brother's keeper; I am my sister's keeper. And that it's not enough to just believe this—we have to do our part to make it a reality. My faith teaches me that I can sit in church and pray all I want, but I won't be fulfilling God's will unless I go out and do the Lord's work.

That's why pastors, friends of mine like Rick Warren and T.D. Jakes and organizations like World Vision and Catholic Charities are wielding their enormous influence to confront poverty, HIV/AIDS, and the genocide in Darfur. Religious leaders like my friends Rev. Jim Wallis and Rabbi David Saperstein and Nathan Diament are working for justice and fighting for change. And all across the country, communities of faith are sponsoring day care programs, building senior centers, and in so many other ways, taking part in the project of American renewal.

Yet what we also understand is that our values should express themselves not just through our churches or synagogues, temples or mosques; they should express themselves through our government. Because whether it's poverty or racism, the uninsured or the unemployed, war or peace, the challenges we face today are not simply technical problems in search of the perfect ten-point plan. They are moral problems, rooted in both societal indifference and individual callousness—in the imperfections of man.

And so long as we're not doing everything in our personal and collective power to solve them, we know the conscience of our nation cannot rest.

Our conscience can't rest so long as 37 million Americans are poor and forgotten by their leaders in Washington and by the media elites. We need to heed the biblical call to care for "the least of these" and lift the poor out of despair. That's why I've been fighting to expand the Earned Income Tax Credit and the minimum wage. If you're working forty hours a week, you shouldn't be living in poverty. But we also know that government initiatives are not enough. Each of us in our own lives needs to do what we can to help the poor. And until we do, our conscience cannot rest.

Our conscience cannot rest so long as nearly 45 million Americans don't have health insurance and the millions more who do are going bankrupt trying to pay for it. I have made a solemn pledge that I will sign a universal health care bill into law by the end of my first term as president that will cover every American and cut the cost of a typical family's premiums by up to $2500 a year. That's not simply a matter of policy or ideology—it's a moral commitment.

And until we stop the genocide that's being carried out in Darfur as I speak, our conscience cannot rest. This is a problem that's brought together churches and synagogues and mosques and people of all faiths as part of a grassroots movement. Universities and states, including Illinois, are taking part in a divestment campaign to pressure the Sudanese government to stop the killings. It's not enough, but it's helping. And it's a testament to what we can achieve when good people with strong convictions stand up for their beliefs.

And we should close Guantanamo Bay and stop tolerating the torture of our enemies. Because it's not who we are. It's not consistent with our traditions of justice and fairness. And it offends our conscience.

But we also know our conscience cannot rest so long as the war goes on in Iraq. It's a war I'm proud I opposed from the start—a war that should never have been authorized and never been waged. I have a plan that would have already begun redeploying our troops with the goal of bringing all our combat brigades home by March 31st of next year. The President vetoed a similar plan, but he doesn't have the last word, and we're going to keep at it, until we bring this war to an end. Because the Iraq war is not just a security problem, it's a moral problem.

And there's another issue we must confront as well. Today there are 12 million undocumented immigrants in America, most of them working in our communities, attending our churches, and contributing to our country.

Now, as children of God, we believe in the worth and dignity of every human being; it doesn't matter where that person came from or what documents they have. We believe that everyone, everywhere should be loved, and given the chance to work, and raise a family.

But as Americans, we also know that this is a nation of laws, and we cannot have those laws broken when more than 2,000 people cross our borders illegally every day. We cannot ignore that we have a right and a duty to protect our borders. And we cannot ignore the very real concerns of Americans who are not worried about illegal immigration because they are racist or xenophobic, but because they fear it will result in lower wages when they're already struggling to raise their families.

And so this will be a difficult debate next week. Consensus and compromise will not come easy. Last time we took up immigration reform, it failed. But we cannot walk away this time. Our conscience cannot rest until we not only secure our borders, but give the 12 million undocumented immigrants in this country a chance to earn their citizenship by paying a fine and waiting in line behind all those who came here legally.

We will all have to make concessions to achieve this. That's what compromise is about. But at the end of the day, we cannot walk away—not for the sake of passing a bill, but so that we can finally address the real concerns of Americans and the persistent hopes of all those brothers and sisters who want nothing more than their own chance at our common dream.

These are some of the challenges that test our conscience—as Americans and people of faith. And meeting them won't be easy. There is real evil and hardship and pain and suffering in the world and we should be humble in our belief that we can eliminate them. But we shouldn't use our humility as an excuse for inaction. We shouldn't use the obstacles we face as an excuse for cynicism. We have to do what we can, knowing it's hard and not swinging from a naïve idealism to a bitter defeatism—but rather, accepting the fact that we're not going to solve every problem overnight, but we can still make a difference.

We can recognize the truth that's at the heart of the UCC: that the conversation is not over; that our roles are not defined; that through ancient texts and modern voices, God is still speaking, challenging us to change not just our own lives, but the world around us.

I'm hearing from evangelicals who may not agree with progressives on every issue but agree that poverty has no place in a world of plenty; that hate has no place in the hearts of believers; and that we all have to be good stewards of God's creations. From Willow Creek to the 'emerging church,' from the Southern Baptist Convention to the National Association of Evangelicals, folks are realizing that the four walls of the church are too small for a big God. God is still speaking.

I'm hearing from progressives who understand that if we want to communicate our hopes and values to Americans, we can't abandon the field of religious discourse. That's why organizations are rising up across the country to reclaim the language of faith to bring about change. God is still speaking.

He's still speaking to our Catholic friends—who are holding up a consistent ethic of life that goes beyond abortion—one that includes a respect for life and dignity whether it's in Iraq, in poor neighborhoods, in African villages or even on death row. They're telling me that their conversation about what it means to be Catholic continues. God is still speaking.

And right here in the UCC, we're hearing from God about what it means to be a welcoming church that holds on to our Christian witness. The UCC is still listening. And God is still speaking.

Now, some of you may have heard me talk about the Joshua generation. But there's a story I want to share that takes place before Moses passed the mantle of leadership on to Joshua. It comes from Deuteronomy 30 when Moses talks to his followers about the challenges they'll find when they reach the Promised Land without him. To the Joshua generation, these challenges seem momentous—and they are. But Moses says: What I am commanding you is not too difficult for you or beyond your reach. It is not up in heaven. Nor is it beyond the sea. No, the word is very near. It is on your lips and in your heart.

It's an idea that's often forgotten or dismissed in cynical times. It's that we all have it within our power to make this a better world. Because we all have the capacity to do justice and show mercy; to treat others with dignity and respect; and to rise above what divides us and come together to meet those challenges we can't meet alone. It's the wisdom Moses imparted to those who would succeed him. And it's a lesson we need to remember today—as members of another Joshua generation.

So let's rededicate ourselves to a new kind of politics—a politics of conscience. Let's come together—Protestant and Catholic, Muslim and Hindu and Jew, believer and non-believer alike. We're not going to agree on everything, but we can disagree without being disagreeable. We can affirm our faith without endangering the separation of church and state, as long as we understand that when we're in the public square, we have to speak in universal terms that everyone can understand. And if we can do that—if we can embrace a common destiny—then I believe we'll not just help bring about a more hopeful day in America, we'll not just be caring for our own souls, we'll be doing God's work here on Earth. Thank you.

U.S. Senator Barack Obama: "Our Moment is Now"

Des Moines, IA

December 27, 2007

*T*en months ago, I stood on the steps of the Old State Capitol in Springfield, Illinois, and began an unlikely journey to change America.

I did not run for the presidency to fulfill some long-held ambition or because I believed it was somehow owed to me. I chose to run in this election—at this moment—because of what Dr. King called "the fierce urgency of now." Because we are at a defining moment in our history. Our nation is at war. Our planet is in peril. Our health care system is broken, our economy is out of balance, our education system fails too many of our children, and our retirement system is in tatters.

At this defining moment, we cannot wait any longer for universal health care. We cannot wait to fix our schools. We cannot wait for good jobs, and living wages, and pensions we can count on. We cannot wait to halt global warming, and we cannot wait to end this war in Iraq.

I chose to run because I believed that the size of these challenges had outgrown the capacity of our broken and divided politics to solve them; because I believed that Americans of every political stripe were hungry for a new kind of politics, a politics that focused not just on how to win but why we should, a politics that focused on those values and ideals that we held in common as Americans; a politics that favored common sense over ideology, straight talk over spin.

Most of all, I believed in the power of the American people to be the real agents of change in this country—because we are not as divided as our politics suggests; because we are a decent, generous people willing to work hard and sacrifice for future generations; and I was certain that if we could just mobilize our voices to challenge the special interests that dominate Washington and challenge ourselves to reach for something better, there was no problem we couldn't solve—no destiny we couldn't fulfill.

Ten months later, Iowa, you have vindicated that faith. You've come out in the blistering heat and the bitter cold not just to cheer, but to challenge—to ask the tough questions; to lift the hood and kick the tires; to serve as one place in America where someone who hasn't spent their life in the Washington spotlight can get a fair hearing.

You've earned the role you play in our democracy because no one takes it more seriously. And I believe that's true this year more than ever because, like me, you feel that same sense of urgency.

All across this state, you've shared with me your stories. And all too often they've been stories of struggle and hardship.

I've heard from seniors who were betrayed by CEOs who dumped their pensions while pocketing bonuses, and from those who still can't afford their prescriptions because Congress refused to negotiate with the drug companies for the cheapest available price.

I've met Maytag workers who labored all their lives only to see their jobs shipped overseas; who now compete with their teenagers for $7-an-hour jobs at Wal-Mart.

I've spoken with teachers who are working at donut shops after school just to make ends meet; who are still digging into their own pockets to pay for school supplies.

Just two weeks ago, I heard a young woman in Cedar Rapids who told me she only gets three hours of sleep because she works the night shift after a full day of college and still can't afford health care for a sister with cerebral palsy. She spoke not with self-pity but with determination, and wonders why the government isn't doing more to help her afford the education that will allow her to live out her dreams.

I've spoken to veterans who talk with pride about what they've accomplished in Afghanistan and Iraq, but who nevertheless think of those they've left behind and question the wisdom of our mission in Iraq; the mothers weeping in my arms over the memories of their sons; the disabled or homeless vets who wonder why their service has been forgotten.

And I've spoken to Americans in every corner of the state, patriots all, who wonder why we have allowed our standing in the world to decline so badly, so quickly. They know this has not made us safer. They know that we must never negotiate out of fear, but that we must never fear to negotiate with our enemies as well as our friends. They are ashamed of Abu Graib and Guantanamo and warrantless wiretaps and ambiguity on torture. They love their country and want its cherished values and ideals restored.

It is precisely because you've experience these frustrations, and seen the cost of inaction in your own lives, that you understand why we can't afford to settle for the same old politics. You know that we can't afford to allow the insurance lobbyists to kill health care reform one more time, and the oil lobbyists to keep us addicted to fossil fuels because no one stood up and took their power away when they had the chance.

You know that we can't afford four more years of the same divisive food fight in Washington that's about scoring political points instead of solving problems; that's about tearing your opponents down instead of lifting this country up.

We can't afford the same politics of fear that tells Democrats that the only way to look tough on national security is to talk, act, and vote like George Bush Republicans; that invokes 9/11 as a way to scare up votes instead of a challenge that should unite all Americans to defeat our real enemies.

We can't afford to be so worried about losing the next election that we lose the battles we owe to the next generation.

The real gamble in this election is playing the same Washington game with the same Washington players and expecting a different result. And that's a risk we can't take. Not this year. Not when the stakes are this high.

In this election, it is time to turn the page. In seven days, it is time to stand for change.

This has been our message since the beginning of this campaign. It was our message when we were down, and our message when we were up. And it must be catching on, because in these last few weeks, everyone is talking about change.

But you can't at once argue that you're the master of a broken system in Washington and offer yourself as the person to change it. You can't fall in line behind the conventional thinking on issues as profound as war and offer yourself as the leader who is best prepared to chart a new and better course for America.

The truth is, you can have the right kind of experience and the wrong kind of experience. Mine is rooted in the real lives of real people and it will bring real results if we have the courage to change. I believe deeply in those words. But they are not mine. They were Bill Clinton's in 1992, when Washington insiders questioned his readiness to lead.

My experience is rooted in the lives of the men and women on the South Side of Chicago who I fought for as an organizer when the local steel plant closed. It's rooted in the lives of the people I stood up for as a civil rights lawyer when they were denied opportunity on the job or justice at the voting booth because of what they looked like or where they came from. It's rooted in an understanding of how the world sees America that I gained from living, traveling, and having family beyond our shores—an understanding that led me to oppose this war in Iraq from the start. It's experience rooted in the real lives of real people, and it's the kind of experience Washington needs right now.

There are others in this race who say that this kind of change sounds good, but that I'm not angry or confrontational enough to get it done.

Well, let me tell you something, Iowa. I don't need any lectures on how to bring about change, because I haven't just talked about it on the campaign trail. I've fought for change all my life.

I walked away from a job on Wall Street to bring job training to the jobless and after school programs to kids on the streets of Chicago.

I turned down the big money law firms to win justice for the powerless as a civil rights lawyer.

I took on the lobbyists in Illinois and brought Democrats and Republicans together to expand health care to 150,000 people and pass the first major campaign finance reform in twenty-five years; and I did the same thing in Washington when we passed the toughest lobbying reform since Watergate. I'm the only candidate in this race who hasn't just talked about taking power away from lobbyists, I've actually done it. So if you want to know what kind of choices we'll make as President, you should take a look at the choices we made when we had the chance to bring about change that wasn't easy or convenient.

That's the kind of change that's more than just rhetoric—that's change you can believe in.

It's change that won't just come from more anger at Washington or turning up the heat on Republicans. There's no shortage of anger and bluster and bitter partisanship out there. We don't need more heat. We need more light. I've learned in my life that you can stand firm in your principles while still reaching out to those who might not always agree with you. And although the Republican operatives in Washington might not be interested in hearing what we have to say, I think Republican and independent voters outside of Washington are. That's the once-in-a-generation opportunity we have in this election.

For the first time in a long time, we have the chance to build a new majority of not just Democrats, but Independents and Republicans who've lost faith in their Washington leaders but want to believe again—who desperately want something new.

We can change the electoral math that's been all about division and make it about addition—about building a coalition for change and progress that stretches through Blue States and Red States. That's how I won some of the reddest, most Republican counties in Illinois. That's why the polls show that I do best against the Republicans running for President—because we're attracting more support from Independents and Republicans than any other candidate. That's how we'll win in November and that's how we'll change this country over the next four years.

In the end, the argument we are having between the candidates in the last seven days is not just about the meaning of change. It's about the meaning of hope. Some of my opponents appear scornful of the word; they think it speaks of naivete, passivity, and wishful thinking.

But that's not what hope is. Hope is not blind optimism. It's not ignoring the enormity of the task before us or the roadblocks that stand in our path. Yes, the lobbyists will fight us. Yes, the Republican attack dogs will go after us in the general election. Yes, the problems of poverty and climate change and failing schools will resist easy repair. I know—I've been on the streets, I've been in the courts. I've watched legislation die because the powerful held sway and good intentions weren't fortified by political will, and I've watched a nation get mislead into war because no one had the judgment or the courage to ask the hard questions before we sent our troops to fight.

But I also know this. I know that hope has been the guiding force behind the most improbable changes this country has ever made. In the face of tyranny, it's what led a band of colonists to rise up against an Empire. In the face of slavery, it's what fueled the resistance of the slave and the abolitionist, and what allowed a President to chart a treacherous course to ensure that the nation would not continue half slave and half free. In the face of war and Depression, it's what led the greatest of generations to free a continent and heal a nation. In the face of oppression, it's what led young men and women to sit at lunch counters and brave fire hoses and march through the streets of Selma and Montgomery for freedom's cause. That's the power of hope—to imagine, and then work for, what had seemed impossible before.

That's the change we seek. And that's the change you can stand for in seven days.

We've already beaten odds that the cynics said couldn't be beaten. When we started ten months ago, they said we couldn't run a different kind of campaign.

They said we couldn't compete without taking money from Washington lobbyists. But you proved them wrong when we raised more small donations from more Americans than any other campaign in history. They said we couldn't be successful if we didn't have the full support of the establishment in Washington. But you proved them wrong when we built a grassroots movement that could forever change the face of American politics.

They said we wouldn't have a chance in this campaign unless we resorted to the same old negative attacks. But we resisted, even when we were written off, and ran a positive campaign that pointed out real differences and rejected the politics of slash and burn.

And now, in seven days, you have a chance once again to prove the cynics wrong. In seven days, what was improbable has the chance to beat what Washington said was inevitable. And that's why in these last weeks, Washington is fighting back with everything it has—with attack ads and insults; with distractions and dishonesty; with millions of dollars from outside groups and undisclosed donors to try and block our path.

We've seen this script many times before. But I know that this time can be different.

Because I know that when the American people believe in something, it happens.

If you believe, then we can tell the lobbyists that their days of setting the agenda in Washington are over.

If you believe, then we can stop making promises to America's workers and start delivering—jobs that pay, health care that's affordable, pensions you can count on, and a tax cut for working Americans instead of the companies who send their jobs overseas .

If you believe, we can offer a world-class education to every child, and pay our teachers more, and make college dreams a reality for every American.

If you believe, we can save this planet and end our dependence on foreign oil.

If you believe, we can end this war, close Guantanamo, restore our standing, renew our diplomacy, and once again respect the Constitution of the United States of America .

That's the future within our reach. That's what hope is—that thing inside us that insists, despite all evidence to the contrary, that something better is waiting for us around the corner. But only if we're willing to work for it and fight for it. To shed our fears and our doubts and our cynicism. To glory in the task before us of remaking this country block by block, precinct by precinct, county by county, state by state.

There is a moment in the life of every generation when, if we are to make our mark on history, this spirit must break through

This is the moment.

This is our time.

And if you will stand with me in seven days—if you will stand for change so that our children have the same chance that somebody gave us; if you'll stand to keep the American dream alive for those who still hunger for opportunity and thirst for justice; if you're ready to stop settling for what the cynics tell you you must accept, and finally reach for what you know is possible, then we will win this caucus, we will win this election, we will change the course of history, and the real journey—to heal a nation and repair the world—will have truly begun.

Thank you.

U.S. Senator Barack Obama: Iowa Caucus Victory Speech

Des Moines, IA

January 3, 2008

ᘓ 95 ᘔ

*T*hank you, Iowa.

You know, they said this day would never come.

They said our sights were set too high.

They said this country was too divided; too disillusioned to ever come together around a common purpose.

But on this January night—at this defining moment in history—you have done what the cynics said we couldn't do. You have done what the state of New Hampshire can do in five days. You have done what America can do in this New Year, 2008. In lines that stretched around schools and churches; in small towns and big cities; you came together as Democrats, Republicans and Independents to stand up and say that we are one nation; we are one people; and our time for change has come.

You said the time has come to move beyond the bitterness and pettiness and anger that's consumed Washington; to end the political strategy that's been all about division and instead make it about addition—to build a coalition for change that stretches through Red States and Blue States. Because that's how we'll win in November, and that's how we'll finally meet the challenges that we face as a nation.

We are choosing hope over fear. We're choosing unity over division, and sending a powerful message that change is coming to America.

You said the time has come to tell the lobbyists who think their money and their influence speak louder than our voices that they don't own this government, we do; and we are here to take it back.

The time has come for a President who will be honest about the choices and the challenges we face; who will listen to you and learn from you even when we disagree; who won't just tell you what you want to hear, but what you need to know. And in New Hampshire, if you give me the same chance that Iowa did tonight, I will be that president for America.

Thank you.

I'll be a President who finally makes health care affordable and available to every single American the same way I expanded health care in Illinois—by—by bringing Democrats and Republicans together to get the job done.

I'll be a President who ends the tax breaks for companies that ship our jobs overseas and put a middle-class tax cut into the pockets of the working Americans who deserve it.

I'll be a President who harnesses the ingenuity of farmers and scientists and entrepreneurs to free this nation from the tyranny of oil once and for all.

And I'll be a President who ends this war in Iraq and finally brings our troops home; who restores our moral standing; who understands that 9/11 is not a way to scare up votes, but a challenge that should unite America and the world against the common threats of the twenty-first century; common threats of terrorism and nuclear weapons; climate change and poverty; genocide and disease.

Tonight, we are one step closer to that vision of America because of what you did here in Iowa. And so I'd especially like to thank the organizers and the precinct captains; the volunteers and the staff who made this all possible.

And while I'm at it, on "thank yous," I think it makes sense for me to thank the love of my life, the rock of the Obama family, the closer on the campaign trail; give it up for Michelle Obama.

I know you didn't do this for me. You did this-you did this because you believed so deeply in the most American of ideas—that in the face of impossible odds, people who love this country can change it.

I know this-I know this because while I may be standing here tonight, I'll never forget that my journey began on the streets of Chicago doing what so many of you have done for this campaign and all the campaigns here in Iowa—organizing, and working, and fighting to make people's lives just a little bit better.

I know how hard it is. It comes with little sleep, little pay, and a lot of sacrifice. There are days of disappointment, but sometimes, just sometimes, there are nights like this—a night-a night that, years from now, when we've made the changes we believe in; when more families can afford to see a doctor; when our children-when Malia and Sasha and your children-inherit a planet that's a little cleaner and safer; when the world sees America differently, and America sees itself as a nation less divided and more united; you'll be able to look back with pride and say that this was the moment when it all began.

This was the moment when the improbable beat what Washington always said was inevitable.

This was the moment when we tore down barriers that have divided us for too long—when we rallied people of all parties and ages to a common cause; when we finally gave Americans who'd never participated in politics a reason to stand up and to do so.

This was the moment when we finally beat back the politics of fear, and doubt, and cynicism; the politics where we tear each other down instead of lifting this country up. This was the moment.

Years from now, you'll look back and you'll say that this was the moment—this was the place—where America remembered what it means to hope.

For many months, we've been teased, even derided for talking about hope.

But we always knew that hope is not blind optimism. It's not ignoring the enormity of the task ahead or the roadblocks that stand in our path. It's not sitting on the sidelines or shirking from a fight. Hope is that thing inside us that insists, despite all evidence to the contrary, that something better awaits us if we have the courage to reach for it, and to work for it, and to fight for it.

Hope is what I saw in the eyes of the young woman in Cedar Rapids who works the night shift after a full day of college and still can't afford health care for a sister who's ill; a young woman who still believes that this country will give her the chance to live out her dreams.

Hope is what I heard in the voice of the New Hampshire woman who told me that she hasn't been able to breathe since her nephew left for Iraq; who still goes to bed each night praying for his safe return.

Hope is what led a band of colonists to rise up against an empire; what led the greatest of generations to free a continent and heal a nation; what led young women and young men to sit at lunch counters and brave fire hoses and march through Selma and Montgomery for freedom's cause.

Hope-hope-is what led me here today—with a father from Kenya; a mother from Kansas; and a story that could only happen in the United States of America. Hope is the bedrock of this nation; the belief that our destiny will not be written for us, but by us; by all those men and women who are not content to settle for the world as it is; who have the courage to remake the world as it should be.

That is what we started here in Iowa, and that is the message we can now carry to New Hampshire and beyond; the same message we had when we were up and when we were down; the one that can change this country brick by brick, block by block, calloused hand by calloused hand—that together, ordinary people can do extraordinary things; because we are not a collection of Red States and Blue States, we are the United States of America; and at this moment, in this election, we are ready to believe again. Thank you, Iowa.

U.S. Senator Barack Obama: New Hampshire Primary Speech After Loss

Nashua, NH

January 8, 2008

I want to congratulate Senator Clinton on a hard-fought victory here in New Hampshire.

A few weeks ago, no one imagined that we'd have accomplished what we did here tonight. For most of this campaign, we were far behind, and we always knew our climb would be steep.

But in record numbers, you came out and spoke up for change. And with your voices and your votes, you made it clear that at this moment – in this election – there is something happening in America.

There is something happening when men and women in Des Moines and Davenport; in Lebanon and Concord come out in the snows of January to wait in lines that stretch block after block because they believe in what this country can be.

There is something happening when Americans who are young in age and in spirit – who have never before participated in politics – turn out in numbers we've never seen because they know in their hearts that this time must be different.

There is something happening when people vote not just for the party they belong to but the hopes they hold in common – that whether we are rich or poor; black or white; Latino or Asian; whether we hail from Iowa or New Hampshire, Nevada or South Carolina, we are ready to take this country in a fundamentally new direction. That is what's happening in America right now. Change is what's happening in America.

You can be the new majority who can lead this nation out of a long political darkness – Democrats, Independents and Republicans who are tired of the division and distraction that has clouded Washington; who know that we can disagree without being disagreeable; who understand that if we mobilize our voices to challenge the money and influence that's stood in our way and challenge ourselves to reach for something better, there's no problem we can't solve – no destiny we cannot fulfill.

Our new American majority can end the outrage of unaffordable, unavailable health care in our time. We can bring doctors and patients; workers and businesses, Democrats and Republicans together; and we can tell the drug and insurance industry that while they'll get a seat at the table, they don't get to buy every chair. Not this time. Not now.

Our new majority can end the tax breaks for corporations that ship our jobs overseas and put a middle-class tax cut into the pockets of the working Americans who deserve it.

We can stop sending our children to schools with corridors of shame and start putting them on a pathway to success. We can stop talking about how great teachers are and start rewarding them for their greatness. We can do this with our new majority.

We can harness the ingenuity of farmers and scientists; citizens and entrepreneurs to free this nation from the tyranny of oil and save our planet from a point of no return.

And when I am President, we will end this war in Iraq and bring our troops home; we will finish the job against al Qaeda in Afghanistan; we will care for our veterans; we will restore our moral standing in the world; and we will never use 9/11 as a way to scare up votes, because it is not a tactic to win an election, it is a challenge that should unite America and the world against the common threats of the twenty-first century: terrorism and nuclear weapons; climate change and poverty; genocide and disease.

All of the candidates in this race share these goals. All have good ideas. And all are patriots who serve this country honorably.

But the reason our campaign has always been different is because it's not just about what I will do as President, it's also about what you, the people who love this country, can do to change it.

That's why tonight belongs to you. It belongs to the organizers and the volunteers and the staff who believed in our improbable journey and rallied so many others to join.

We know the battle ahead will be long, but always remember that no matter what obstacles stand in our way, nothing can withstand the power of millions of voices calling for change.

We have been told we cannot do this by a chorus of cynics who will only grow louder and more dissonant in the weeks to come. We've been asked to pause for a reality check. We've been warned against offering the people of this nation false hope.

But in the unlikely story that is America, there has never been anything false about hope. For when we have faced down impossible odds; when we've been told that we're not ready, or that we shouldn't try, or that we can't, generations of Americans have responded with a simple creed that sums up the spirit of a people.

Yes we can.

It was a creed written into the founding documents that declared the destiny of a nation.

Yes we can.

It was whispered by slaves and abolitionists as they blazed a trail toward freedom through the darkest of nights.

Yes we can.

It was sung by immigrants as they struck out from distant shores and pioneers who pushed westward against an unforgiving wilderness.

Yes we can.

It was the call of workers who organized; women who reached for the ballot; a President who chose the moon as our new frontier; and a King who took us to the mountaintop and pointed the way to the Promised Land.

Yes we can to justice and equality. Yes we can to opportunity and prosperity. Yes we can heal this nation. Yes we can repair this world. Yes we can.

And so tomorrow, as we take this campaign South and West; as we learn that the struggles of the textile worker in Spartanburg are not so different than the plight of the dishwasher in Las Vegas; that the hopes of the little girl who goes to a crumbling school in Dillon are the same as the dreams of the boy who learns on the streets of LA; we will remember that there is something happening in America; that we are not as divided as our politics suggests; that we are one people; we are one nation; and together, we will begin the next great chapter in America's story with three words that will ring from coast to coast; from sea to shining sea – Yes. We. Can.

U.S. Senator Barack Obama: Speech at the Ebenezer Baptist Church[1] "The Great Need of the Hour"

Atlanta, GA

January 20, 2008

---

1   Ebenezer Baptist Church is the church where Martin Luther King, Jr. and his father, Martin Luther King, Sr., pastored.

*T*he Scripture tells us that when Joshua and the Israelites arrived at the gates of Jericho, they could not enter. The walls of the city were too steep for any one person to climb; too strong to be taken down with brute force. And so they sat for days, unable to pass on through.

But God had a plan for his people. He told them to stand together and march together around the city, and on the seventh day he told them that when they heard the sound of the ram's horn, they should speak with one voice. And at the chosen hour, when the horn sounded and a chorus of voices cried out together, the mighty walls of Jericho came tumbling down.

There are many lessons to take from this passage, just as there are many lessons to take from this day, just as there are many memories that fill the space of this church. As I was thinking about which ones we need to remember at this hour, my mind went back to the very beginning of the modern Civil Rights Era.

Because before Memphis and the mountaintop; before the bridge in Selma and the march on Washington; before Birmingham and the beatings; the fire hoses and the loss of those four little girls; before there was King the icon and his magnificent dream, there was King the young preacher and a people who found themselves suffering under the yoke of oppression.

And on the eve of the bus boycotts in Montgomery, at a time when many were still doubtful about the possibilities of change, a time when those in the black community mistrusted themselves, and at times mistrusted each other, King inspired with words not of anger, but of an urgency that still speaks to us today:

"Unity is the great need of the hour" is what King said. Unity is how we shall overcome.

What Dr. King understood is that if just one person chose to walk instead of ride the bus, those walls of oppression would not be moved. But maybe if a few more walked, the foundation might start to shake. If a few more women were willing to do what Rosa Parks had done, maybe the cracks would start to show. If teenagers took freedom rides from North to South, maybe a few bricks would come loose. Maybe if white folks marched because they had come to understand that their freedom too was at stake in the impending battle, the wall would begin to sway. And if enough Americans were awakened to the injustice; if they joined together, North and South, rich and poor, Christian and Jew, then perhaps that wall would come tumbling down, and justice would flow like water, and righteousness like a mighty stream.

Unity is the great need of the hour—the great need of this hour. Not because it sounds pleasant or because it makes us feel good, but because it's the only way we can overcome the essential deficit that exists in this country.

I'm not talking about a budget deficit. I'm not talking about a trade deficit. I'm not talking about a deficit of good ideas or new plans.

I'm talking about a moral deficit. I'm talking about an empathy deficit. I'm taking about an inability to recognize ourselves in one another; to understand that we are our brother's keeper; we are our sister's keeper; that, in the words of Dr. King, we are all tied together in a single garment of destiny.

We have an empathy deficit when we're still sending our children down corridors of shame—schools in the forgotten corners of America where the color of your skin still affects the content of your education.

We have a deficit when CEOs are making more in ten minutes than some workers make in ten months; when families lose their homes so that lenders make a profit; when mothers can't afford a doctor when their children get sick.

We have a deficit in this country when there is Scooter Libby justice for some and Jena justice for others; when our children see nooses hanging from a schoolyard tree today, in the present, in the twenty-first century.

We have a deficit when homeless veterans sleep on the streets of our cities; when innocents are slaughtered in the deserts of Darfur; when young Americans serve tour after tour of duty in a war that should've never been authorized and never been waged.

And we have a deficit when it takes a breach in our levees to reveal a breach in our compassion; when it takes a terrible storm to reveal the hungry that God calls on us to feed; the sick He calls on us to care for; the least of these He commands that we treat as our own.

So we have a deficit to close. We have walls—barriers to justice and equality—that must come down. And to do this, we know that unity is the great need of this hour.

Unfortunately, all too often when we talk about unity in this country, we've come to believe that it can be purchased on the cheap. We've come to believe that racial reconciliation can come easily—that it's just a matter of a few ignorant people trapped in the prejudices of the past, and that if the demagogues and those who exploit our racial divisions will simply go away, then all our problems would be solved.

All too often, we seek to ignore the profound institutional barriers that stand in the way of ensuring opportunity for all children, or decent jobs for all people, or health care for those who are sick. We long for unity, but are unwilling to pay the price.

But of course, true unity cannot be so easily won. It starts with a change in attitudes—a broadening of our minds, and a broadening of our hearts.

It's not easy to stand in somebody else's shoes. It's not easy to see past our differences. We've all encountered this in our own lives. But what makes it even more difficult is that we have a politics in this country that seeks to drive us apart—that puts up walls between us.

We are told that those who differ from us on a few things are different from us on all things; that our problems are the fault of those who don't think like us or look like us or come from where we do. The welfare queen is taking our tax money. The immigrant is taking our jobs. The believer condemns the non-believer as immoral, and the non-believer chides the believer as intolerant.

For most of this country's history, we in the African-American community have been at the receiving end of man's inhumanity to man. And all of us understand intimately the insidious role that race still sometimes plays—on the job, in the schools, in our health care system, and in our criminal justice system.

And yet, if we are honest with ourselves, we must admit that none of our hands are entirely clean. If we're honest with ourselves, we'll acknowledge that our own community has not always been true to King's vision of a beloved community.

We have scorned our gay brothers and sisters instead of embracing them. The scourge of anti-Semitism has, at times, revealed itself in our community. For too long, some of us have seen immigrants as competitors for jobs instead of companions in the fight for opportunity.

Every day, our politics fuels and exploits this kind of division across all races and regions; across gender and party. It is played out on television. It is sensationalized by the media. And last week, it even crept into the campaign for President, with charges and counter-charges that served to obscure the issues instead of illuminating the critical choices we face as a nation.

So let us say that on this day of all days, each of us carries with us the task of changing our hearts and minds. The division, the stereotypes, the scape-goating, the ease with which we blame our plight on others—all of this distracts us from the common challenges we face—war and poverty; injustice and inequality. We can no longer afford to build ourselves up by tearing someone else down. We can no longer afford to traffic in lies or fear or hate. It is the poison that we must purge from our politics; the wall that we must tear down before the hour grows too late.

Because if Dr. King could love his jailor; if he could call on the faithful who once sat where you do to forgive those who set dogs and fire hoses upon them, then surely we can look past what divides us in our time, and bind up our wounds, and erase the empathy deficit that exists in our hearts.

But if changing our hearts and minds is the first critical step, we cannot stop there. It is not enough to bemoan the plight of poor children in this country and remain unwilling to push our elected officials to provide the resources to fix our schools. It is not enough to decry the disparities of health care and yet allow the insurance companies and the drug companies to block much-needed reforms. It is not enough for us to abhor the costs of a misguided war, and yet allow ourselves to be driven by a politics of fear that sees the threat of attack as way to scare up votes instead of a call to come together around a common effort.

The Scripture tells us that we are judged not just by word, but by deed. And if we are to truly bring about the unity that is so crucial in this time, we must find it within ourselves to act on what we know; to understand that living up to this country's ideals and its possibilities will require great effort and resources; sacrifice and stamina.

And that is what is at stake in the great political debate we are having today. The changes that are needed are not just a matter of tinkering at the edges, and they will not come if politicians simply tell us what we want to hear. All of us will be called upon to make some sacrifice. None of us will be exempt from responsibility. We will have to fight to fix our schools, but we will also have to challenge ourselves to be better parents. We will have to confront the biases in our criminal justice system, but we will also have to acknowledge the deep-seated violence that still resides in our own communities and marshal the will to break its grip.

That is how we will bring about the change we seek. That is how Dr. King led this country through the wilderness. He did it with words—words that he spoke not just to the children of slaves, but the children of slave owners. Words that inspired not just black but also white; not just the Christian but the Jew; not just the Southerner but also the Northerner.

He led with words, but he also led with deeds. He also led by example. He led by marching and going to jail and suffering threats and being away from his family. He led by taking a stand against a war, knowing full well that it would diminish his popularity. He led by challenging our economic structures, understanding that it would cause discomfort. Dr. King understood that unity cannot be won on the cheap; that we would have to earn it through great effort and determination.

That is the unity—the hard-earned unity—that we need right now. It is that effort, and that determination, that can transform blind optimism into hope—the hope to imagine, and work for, and fight for what seemed impossible before.

The stories that give me such hope don't happen in the spotlight. They don't happen on the presidential stage. They happen in the quiet corners of our lives. They happen in the moments we least expect. Let me give you an example of one of those stories.

There is a young, twenty-three year old white woman named Ashley Baia who organizes for our campaign in Florence, South Carolina. She's been working to organize a mostly African-American community since the beginning of this campaign, and the other day she was at a roundtable discussion where everyone went around telling their story and why they were there.

And Ashley said that when she was nine years old, her mother got cancer. And because she had to miss days of work, she was let go and lost her health care. They had to file for bankruptcy, and that's when Ashley decided that she had to do something to help her mom.

She knew that food was one of their most expensive costs, and so Ashley convinced her mother that what she really liked and really wanted to eat more than anything else was mustard and relish sandwiches. Because that was the cheapest way to eat.

She did this for a year until her mom got better, and she told everyone at the roundtable that the reason she joined our campaign was so that she could help the millions of other children in the country who want and need to help their parents too.

So Ashley finishes her story and then goes around the room and asks everyone else why they're supporting the campaign. They all have different stories and reasons. Many bring up a specific issue. And finally they come to this elderly black man who's been sitting there quietly the entire time. And Ashley asks him why he's there. And he does not bring up a specific issue. He does not say health care or the economy. He does not say education or the war. He does not say that he was there because of Barack Obama. He simply says to everyone in the room, "I am here because of Ashley."

By itself, that single moment of recognition between that young white girl and that old black man is not enough. It is not enough to give health care to the sick, or jobs to the jobless, or education to our children.

But it is where we begin. It is why the walls in that room began to crack and shake.

And if they can shake in that room, they can shake in Atlanta.

And if they can shake in Atlanta, they can shake in Georgia.

And if they can shake in Georgia, they can shake all across America. And if enough of our voices join together; we can bring those walls tumbling down. The walls of Jericho can finally come tumbling down. That is our hope—but only if we pray together, and work together, and march together.

Brothers and sisters, we cannot walk alone.

In the struggle for peace and justice, we cannot walk alone.

In the struggle for opportunity and equality, we cannot walk alone.

In the struggle to heal this nation and repair this world, we cannot walk alone.

So I ask you to walk with me, and march with me, and join your voice with mine, and together we will sing the song that tears down the walls that divide us, and lift up an America that is truly indivisible, with liberty, and justice, for all. May God bless the memory of the great pastor of this church, and may God bless the United States of America.

U.S. Senator Barack Obama: South Carolina Victory Speech

Columbia, SC

January 26, 2008

*O*ver two weeks ago, we saw the people of Iowa proclaim that our time for change has come. But there were those who doubted this country's desire for something new—who said Iowa was a fluke not to be repeated again.

Well, tonight, the cynics who believed that what began in the snows of Iowa was just an illusion were told a different story by the good people of South Carolina.

After four great contests in every corner of this country, we have the most votes, the most delegates, and the most diverse coalition of Americans we've seen in a long, long time.

They are young and old; rich and poor. They are black and white; Latino and Asian. They are Democrats from Des Moines and Independents from Concord; Republicans from rural Nevada and young people across this country who've never had a reason to participate until now. And in nine days, nearly half the nation will have the chance to join us in saying that we are tired of business-as-usual in Washington, we are hungry for change, and we are ready to believe again

But if there's anything we've been reminded of since Iowa, it's that the kind of change we seek will not come easy. Partly because we have fine candidates in the field—fierce competitors, worthy of respect. And as contentious as this campaign may get, we have to remember that this is a contest for the Democratic nomination, and that all of us share an abiding desire to end the disastrous policies of the current administration.

But there are real differences between the candidates. We are looking for more than just a change of party in the White House. We're looking to fundamentally change the status quo in Washington—a status quo that extends beyond any particular party. And right now, that status quo is fighting back with everything it's got; with the same old tactics that divide and distract us from solving the problems people face, whether those problems are health care they can't afford or a mortgage they cannot pay.

So this will not be easy. Make no mistake about what we're up against.

We are up against the belief that it's ok for lobbyists to dominate our government—that they are just part of the system in Washington. But we know that the undue influence of lobbyists is part of the problem, and this election is our chance to say that we're not going to let them stand in our way anymore.

We are up against the conventional thinking that says your ability to lead as President comes from longevity in Washington or proximity to the White House. But we know that real leadership is about candor, and judgment, and the ability to rally Americans from all walks of life around a common purpose—a higher purpose.

We are up against decades of bitter partisanship that cause politicians to demonize their opponents instead of coming together to make college affordable or energy cleaner; it's the kind of partisanship where you're not even allowed to say that a Republican had an idea—even if it's one you never agreed with. That kind of politics is bad for our party, it's bad for our country, and this is our chance to end it once and for all.

We are up against the idea that it's acceptable to say anything and do anything to win an election. We know that this is exactly what's wrong with our politics; this is why people don't believe what their leaders say anymore; this is why they tune out. And this election is our chance to give the American people a reason to believe again.

And what we've seen in these last weeks is that we're also up against forces that are not the fault of any one campaign, but feed the habits that prevent us from being who we want to be as a nation. It's the politics that uses religion as a wedge, and patriotism as a bludgeon. A politics that tells us that we have to think, act, and even vote within the confines of the categories that supposedly define us. The assumption that young people are apathetic. The assumption that Republicans won't cross over. The assumption that the wealthy care nothing for the poor, and that the poor don't vote. The assumption that African-Americans can't support the white candidate; whites can't support the African-American candidate; blacks and Latinos can't come together.

But we are here tonight to say that this is not the America we believe in. I did not travel around this state over the last year and see a white South Carolina or a black South Carolina. I saw South Carolina. I saw crumbling schools that are stealing the future of black children and white children. I saw shuttered mills and homes for sale that once belonged to Americans from all walks of life, and men and women of every color and creed who serve together, and fight together, and bleed together under the same proud flag. I saw what America is, and I believe in what this country can be.

That is the country I see. That is the country you see. But now it is up to us to help the entire nation embrace this vision. Because in the end, we are not just up against the ingrained and destructive habits of Washington, we are also struggling against our own doubts, our own fears, and our own cynicism. The change we seek has always required great struggle and sacrifice. And so this is a battle in our own hearts and minds about what kind of country we want and how hard we're willing to work for it.

So let me remind you tonight that change will not be easy. That change will take time. There will be setbacks, and false starts, and sometimes we will make mistakes. But as hard as it may seem, we cannot lose hope. Because there are people all across this country who are counting us; who can't afford another four years without health care or good schools or decent wages because our leaders couldn't come together and get it done.

Theirs are the stories and voices we carry on from South Carolina.

The mother who can't get Medicaid to cover all the needs of her sick child—she needs us to pass a health care plan that cuts costs and makes health care available and affordable for every single American.

The teacher who works another shift at Dunkin Donuts after school just to make ends meet—she needs us to reform our education system so that she gets better pay, and more support, and her students get the resources they need to achieve their dreams.

The Maytag worker who is now competing with his own teenager for a $7-an-hour job at Wal-Mart because the factory he gave his life to shut its doors—he needs us to stop giving tax breaks to companies that ship our jobs overseas and start putting them in the pockets of working Americans who deserve it. And struggling homeowners. And seniors who should retire with dignity and respect.

The woman who told me that she hasn't been able to breathe since the day her nephew left for Iraq, or the soldier who doesn't know his child because he's on his third or fourth tour of duty—they need us to come together and put an end to a war that should've never been authorized and never been waged.

The choice in this election is not between regions or religions or genders. It's not about rich versus poor; young versus old; and it is not about black versus white.

It's about the past versus the future.

It's about whether we settle for the same divisions and distractions and drama that passes for politics today, or whether we reach for a politics of common sense, and innovation—a shared sacrifice and shared prosperity.

There are those who will continue to tell us we cannot do this. That we cannot have what we long for. That we are peddling false hopes.

But here's what I know. I know that when people say we can't over-come all the big money and influence in Washington, I think of the elderly woman who sent me a contribution the other day—an envelope that had a money order for $3.01 along with a verse of scripture tucked inside. So don't tell us change isn't possible.

When I hear the cynical talk that blacks and whites and Latinos can't join together and work together, I'm reminded of the Latino brothers and sisters I organized with, and stood with, and fought with side by side for jobs and justice on the streets of Chicago. So don't tell us change can't happen.

When I hear that we'll never overcome the racial divide in our poli-tics, I think about that Republican woman who used to work for Strom Thurmond, who's now devoted to educating inner-city children and who went out onto the streets of South Carolina and knocked on doors for this campaign. Don't tell me we can't change.

Yes we can change.

Yes we can heal this nation.

Yes we can seize our future.

And as we leave this state with a new wind at our backs, and take this journey across the country we love with the message we've carried from the plains of Iowa to the hills of New Hampshire; from the Nevada desert to the South Carolina coast; the same message we had when we were up and when we were down—that out of many, we are one; that while we breathe, we hope; and where we are met with cynicism, and doubt, and those who tell us that we can't, we will respond with that timeless creed that sums up the spirit of a people in three simple words:

Yes. We. Can.

U.S. Senator Barack Obama:

Speech at the

Jefferson-Jackson Dinner

Richmond, VA

February 9, 2008

*I*t has now been one year since we began this campaign for the presidency on the steps of the Old State Capitol in Springfield, Illinois—just me and 15,000 of my closest friends.

At the time, there weren't too many who imagined we'd be standing where we are today. I knew I wouldn't be Washington's favorite candidate. I knew we wouldn't get all the big donors or endorsements right off the bat. I knew I'd be the underdog in every contest from January to June. I knew it wouldn't be easy.

But then something started happening. As we met people in their living rooms and on their farms; in churches and town hall meetings, they all started telling a similar story about the state of our politics today. Whether they're young or old; black or white; Latino or Asian; Democrat, Independent or even Republican, the message is the same:

We are tired of being disappointed by our politics. We are tired of being let down. We're tired of hearing promises made and ten-point plans proposed in the heat of a campaign only to have nothing change when everyone goes back to Washington. Because the lobbyists just write another check. Or because politicians start worrying about how they'll win the next election instead of why they should. Or because they focus on who's up and who's down instead of who matters.

And while Washington is consumed with the same drama and division and distraction, another family puts up a For Sale sign in the front yard. Another factory shuts its doors forever. Another mother declares bankruptcy because she cannot pay her child's medical bills.

And another soldier waves goodbye as he leaves on another tour of duty in a war that should've never been authorized and never been waged. It goes on and on and on, year after year after year.

But in this election—at this moment—Americans are standing up all across the country to say, not this time. Not this year. The stakes are too high and the challenges too great to play the same Washington game with the same Washington players and expect a different result. And today, voters from the West Coast to the Gulf Coast to the heart of America stood up to say that it is time to turn the page. We won Louisiana, and Nebraska, and the state of Washington, and I believe that we can win in Virginia on Tuesday if you're ready to stand for change.

Each of us running for the Democratic nomination agrees on one thing that the other party does not—the next President must end the disastrous policies of George W. Bush. And both Senator Clinton and I have put forth detailed plans and good ideas that would do just that.

But I am running for President because I believe that to actually make change happen—to make this time different than all the rest—we need a leader who can finally move beyond the divisive politics of Washington and bring Democrats, Independents, and Republicans together to get things done. That's how we'll win this election, and that's how we'll change this country when I am President of the United States.

This week we found out that the presumptive nominee of the Republican Party is Senator John McCain. Now, John McCain is a good man, an American hero, and we honor his half century of service to this nation. But in this campaign, he has made the decision to embrace the failed policies George Bush's Washington.

He speaks of a hundred year war in Iraq and sees another on the horizon with Iran. He once opposed George Bush's tax cuts for the wealthiest few who don't need them and didn't ask for them. He said they were too expensive and unwise. And he was absolutely right.

But somewhere along the line, the wheels came off the Straight Talk Express because he now he supports the very same tax cuts he voted against. This is what happens when you spend too long in Washington. Politicians don't say what they mean and they don't mean what they say. And that is why in this election, our party cannot stand for business-as-usual in Washington. The Democratic Party must stand for change.

This fall, we owe the American people a real choice.

It's a choice between debating John McCain about who has the most experience in Washington, or debating him about who's most likely to change Washington. Because that's a debate we can win.

It's a choice between debating John McCain about lobbying reform with a nominee who's taken more money from lobbyists than he has, or doing it with a campaign that hasn't taken a dime of their money because we've been funded by you—the American people.

And it's a choice between taking on John McCain with Republicans and Independents already united against us, or running against him with a campaign that's united Americans of all parties around a common purpose.

There is a reason why the last six polls in a row have shown that I'm the strongest candidate against John McCain. It's because we've done better with Independents in almost every single contest we've had. It's because we've won in more Red States and swing states that the next Democratic nominee needs to win in November.

Virginia Democrats know how important this is. That's how Mark Warner won in this state. That's how Tim Kaine won in this state. That's how Jim Webb won in this state. And if I am your nominee, this is one Democrat who plans to campaign in Virginia and win in Virginia this fall.

We are here to make clear that this election is not between regions or religions or genders. It's not about rich versus poor; young versus old; and it is not about black versus white.

It is about the past versus the future. The Republicans in Washington are already running on the politics of yesterday, which is why our party must be the party of tomorrow. And that is the party I will lead as President of the United States.

I know what it takes to pass health care reform because I've done it—not by demonizing anyone who disagrees with me, but by bringing Democrats and Republicans together to provide health insurance to 150,000 children and parents in Illinois.

And when I am President, we'll pass universal health care not in twenty years, not in ten years, but by the end of my first term in office. But you don't have to take my word for it. Senator Ted Kennedy recently said that he wouldn't have endorsed me if he didn't believe passionately that I will fight for universal health care as President. And if there's someone who knows something about health care, it's Ted Kennedy.

My plan would bring down premiums for the typical family by $2500 a year. We'd ban insurance companies from denying you coverage because of a pre-existing condition. We'd allow every American to get the same kind of health care that members of Congress get for themselves. And the one difference between my plan and Senator Clinton's plan is that she said she'd 'go after' your wages if you don't buy health care. Well I believe the reason people don't have health care isn't because no one's forced them to buy it, it's because no one's made it affordable—and that's why we bring down the cost of health care more than any other plan in this race.

It's also time to bring the cost of living down for working families who are struggling in this economy like never before. They're facing rising costs and falling wages, and we owe it to them to end the Bush-McCain tax cuts for the wealthiest 2% and put a tax cut into the pockets of the families who need it.

That's what I did in Illinois when I brought Democrats and Republicans together to provide $100 million in tax relief to working families and the working poor, and that's the kind of tax relief I'll provide as President.

I will end the tax breaks for companies who ship our jobs overseas and give a middle-class tax break to 95% of working Americans. And homeowners who are struggling. And seniors who deserve to retire with dignity and respect. And I won't wait another ten years to raise the minimum wage in this country—I will raise it to keep pace with inflation every single year.

It's also time to give every child, everywhere, a world-class education, from the day they're born to the day they graduate college. I am only here today because somebody, somewhere, gave my father a ticket to come study in America. Because my mother got the opportunity to put herself through graduate school. Because even though we didn't have much growing up, I got scholarships to go to some of the best schools in the country. That's the chance I believe every child should have.

When I am President, we will give our children the best possible start by investing in early childhood education. We'll stop talking about how great our teachers are, and start rewarding them for their greatness, with better pay and more support. And we will provide every American with a $4,000 a year tax credit that will finally help make a college education affordable and available for all.

And when I am President, this party will be the party that finally makes sure our sons and daughters don't grow up in a century where our economy is weighed down by our addiction to oil; our foreign policy is held hostage to the whims of dictators; and our planet passes a moment of no return.

When I called for higher fuel efficiency standards, I didn't do it in front of an environmental group in California—I did it in front of the automakers in Detroit. Now it was pretty quiet—I didn't get a lot of applause. But we need leadership that tells the American people not just what they want to hear, but what we need to know. That's why I will set the goal of an 80% reduction in carbon emissions by 2050, and we will meet it—with higher fuel standards and new investments in renewable fuels that will create millions of new jobs and entire new industries right here in America.

Finally, it is time to turn the page on eight years of a foreign policy that has made us less safe and less respected in the world. If I am the nominee of this party, John McCain will not be able to say that I agreed with him on voting for the war in Iraq; agreed with him on giving George Bush the benefit of the doubt on Iran; and agree with him in embracing the Bush-Cheney policy of not talking to leaders we don't like. Because that doesn't make us look strong, it makes us look arrogant. John F. Kennedy said that you should never negotiate out of fear, but you should never fear to negotiate. And that's what I will do as President. I don't just want to end this war in Iraq, I want to end the mindset that got us into war. It is time to turn the page.

This is our moment. This is our time for change. Our party—the Democratic Party—has always been at its best when we've led not by polls, but by principle; not by calculation, but by conviction; when we've called all Americans to a common purpose—a higher purpose.

We are the party of Jefferson, who wrote the words that we are still trying to heed—that all of us are created equal—that all of us deserve the chance to pursue our happiness.

We're the party of Jackson, who took back the White House for the people of this country.

We're the party of a man who overcame his own disability to tell us that the only thing we had to fear was fear itself; who faced down fascism and liberated a continent from tyranny.

And we're the party of a young President who asked what we could do for our country, and the challenged us to do it.

That is who we are. That is the Party that we need to be, and can be, if we cast off our doubts, and leave behind our fears, and choose the America that we know is possible. Because there is a moment in the life of every generation, if it is to make its mark on history, when its spirit has to come through, when it must choose the future over the past, when it must make its own change from the bottom up.

This is our moment. This is our message—the same message we had when we were up, and when we were down. The same message that we will carry all the way to the convention. And in seven months time we can realize this promise; we can claim this legacy; we can choose new leadership for America. Because there is nothing we cannot do if the American people decide it is time.

U.S. Senator Barack Obama:

"A More Perfect Union"

(Responding to the Reverend Jeremiah Wright Controversy)

Philadelphia, PA

March 18, 2008

"We the people, in order to form a more perfect union."

Two hundred and twenty one years ago, in a hall that still stands across the street, a group of men gathered and, with these simple words, launched America's improbable experiment in democracy. Farmers and scholars; statesmen and patriots who had traveled across an ocean to escape tyranny and persecution finally made real their declaration of independence at a Philadelphia convention that lasted through the spring of 1787.

The document they produced was eventually signed but ultimately unfinished. It was stained by this nation's original sin of slavery, a question that divided the colonies and brought the convention to a stalemate until the founders chose to allow the slave trade to continue for at least twenty more years, and to leave any final resolution to future generations.

Of course, the answer to the slavery question was already embedded within our Constitution—a Constitution that had at is very core the ideal of equal citizenship under the law; a Constitution that promised its people liberty, and justice, and a union that could be and should be perfected over time.

And yet words on a parchment would not be enough to deliver slaves from bondage, or provide men and women of every color and creed their full rights and obligations as citizens of the United States. What would be needed were Americans in successive generations who were willing to do their part—through protests and struggle, on the streets and in the courts, through a civil war and civil disobedience and always at great risk—to narrow that gap between the promise of our ideals and the reality of their time.

This was one of the tasks we set forth at the beginning of this campaign—to continue the long march of those who came before us, a march for a more just, more equal, more free, more caring and more prosperous America. I chose to run for the presidency at this moment in history because I believe deeply that we cannot solve the challenges of our time unless we solve them together—unless we perfect our union by understanding that we may have different stories, but we hold common hopes; that we may not look the same and we may not have come from the same place, but we all want to move in the same direction—towards a better future for our children and our grandchildren.

This belief comes from my unyielding faith in the decency and generosity of the American people. But it also comes from my own American story.

I am the son of a black man from Kenya and a white woman from Kansas. I was raised with the help of a white grandfather who survived a Depression to serve in Patton's Army during World War II and a white grandmother who worked on a bomber assembly line at Fort Leavenworth while he was overseas. I've gone to some of the best schools in America and lived in one of the world's poorest nations. I am married to a black American who carries within her the blood of slaves and slaveowners—an inheritance we pass on to our two precious daughters. I have brothers, sisters, nieces, nephews, uncles and cousins, of every race and every hue, scattered across three continents, and for as long as I live, I will never forget that in no other country on Earth is my story even possible.

It's a story that hasn't made me the most conventional candidate. But it is a story that has seared into my genetic makeup the idea that this nation is more than the sum of its parts—that out of many, we are truly one.

Throughout the first year of this campaign, against all predictions to the contrary, we saw how hungry the American people were for this message of unity. Despite the temptation to view my candidacy through a purely racial lens, we won commanding victories in states with some of the whitest populations in the country. In South Carolina, where the Confederate Flag still flies, we built a powerful coalition of African Americans and white Americans.

This is not to say that race has not been an issue in the campaign. At various stages in the campaign, some commentators have deemed me either "too black" or "not black enough." We saw racial tensions bubble to the surface during the week before the South Carolina primary. The press has scoured every exit poll for the latest evidence of racial polarization, not just in terms of white and black, but black and brown as well.

And yet, it has only been in the last couple of weeks that the discussion of race in this campaign has taken a particularly divisive turn.

On one end of the spectrum, we've heard the implication that my candidacy is somehow an exercise in affirmative action; that it's based solely on the desire of wide-eyed liberals to purchase racial reconciliation on the cheap. On the other end, we've heard my former pastor, Reverend Jeremiah

Wright, use incendiary language to express views that have the potential not only to widen the racial divide, but views that denigrate both the greatness and the goodness of our nation; that rightly offend white and black alike.

I have already condemned, in unequivocal terms, the statements of Reverend Wright that have caused such controversy. For some, nagging questions remain. Did I know him to be an occasionally fierce critic of American domestic and foreign policy? Of course. Did I ever hear him make remarks that could be considered controversial while I sat in church? Yes. Did I strongly disagree with many of his political views? Absolutely— just as I'm sure many of you have heard remarks from your pastors, priests, or rabbis with which you strongly disagreed.

But the remarks that have caused this recent firestorm weren't simply controversial. They weren't simply a religious leader's effort to speak out against perceived injustice. Instead, they expressed a profoundly distorted view of this country—a view that sees white racism as endemic, and that elevates what is wrong with America above all that we know is right with America; a view that sees the conflicts in the Middle East as rooted primarily in the actions of stalwart allies like Israel, instead of emanating from the perverse and hateful ideologies of radical Islam.

As such, Reverend Wright's comments were not only wrong but divisive, divisive at a time when we need unity; racially charged at a time when we need to come together to solve a set of monumental problems—two wars, a terrorist threat, a falling economy, a chronic health care crisis and potentially devastating climate change; problems that are neither black or white or Latino or Asian, but rather problems that confront us all.

Given my background, my politics, and my professed values and ideals, there will no doubt be those for whom my statements of condemnation are not enough. Why associate myself with Reverend Wright in the first place, they may ask? Why not join another church? And I confess that if all that I knew of Reverend Wright were the snippets of those sermons that have run in an endless loop on the television and You Tube, or if Trinity United Church of Christ conformed to the caricatures being peddled by some commentators, there is no doubt that I would react in much the same way

But the truth is, that isn't all that I know of the man. The man I met more than twenty years ago is a man who helped introduce me to my Christian faith, a man who spoke to me about our obligations to love one another; to care for the sick and lift up the poor. He is a man who served his country as a U.S. Marine; who has studied and lectured at some of the finest universities and seminaries in the country, and who for over thirty years led a church that serves the community by doing God's work here on

Earth—by housing the homeless, ministering to the needy, providing day care services and scholarships and prison ministries, and reaching out to those suffering from HIV/AIDS.

In my first book, Dreams From My Father, I described the experience of my first service at Trinity:

"People began to shout, to rise from their seats and clap and cry out, a forceful wind carrying the reverend's voice up into the rafters....And in that single note—hope!—I heard something else; at the foot of that cross, inside the thousands of churches across the city, I imagined the stories of ordinary black people merging with the stories of David and Goliath, Moses and Pharaoh, the Christians in the lion's den, Ezekiel's field of dry bones. Those stories—of survival, and freedom, and hope—became our story, my story; the blood that had spilled was our blood, the tears our tears; until this black church, on this bright day, seemed once more a vessel carrying the story of a people into future generations and into a larger world. Our trials and triumphs became at once unique and universal, black and more than black; in chronicling our journey, the stories and songs gave us a means to reclaim memories that we didn't need to feel shame about... memories that all people might study and cherish—and with which we could start to rebuild."

That has been my experience at Trinity. Like other predominantly black churches across the country, Trinity embodies the black community in its entirety—the doctor and the welfare mom, the model student and the former gang-banger. Like other black churches, Trinity's services are full of raucous laughter and sometimes bawdy humor. They are full of dancing, clapping, screaming and shouting that may seem jarring to the untrained ear. The church contains in full the kindness and cruelty, the fierce intelligence and the shocking ignorance, the struggles and successes, the love and yes, the bitterness and bias that make up the black experience in America.

And this helps explain, perhaps, my relationship with Reverend Wright. As imperfect as he may be, he has been like family to me. He strengthened my faith, officiated my wedding, and baptized my children. Not once in my conversations with him have I heard him talk about any ethnic group in derogatory terms, or treat whites with whom he interacted with anything but courtesy and respect. He contains within him the contradictions—the good and the bad—of the community that he has served diligently for so many years.

I can no more disown him than I can disown the black community. I can no more disown him than I can my white grandmother—a woman who helped raise me, a woman who sacrificed again and again for me, a woman who loves me as much as she loves anything in this world, but a woman who once confessed her fear of black men who passed by her on the street, and who on more than one occasion has uttered racial or ethnic stereotypes that made me cringe.

These people are a part of me. And they are a part of America, this country that I love.

Some will see this as an attempt to justify or excuse comments that are simply inexcusable. I can assure you it is not. I suppose the politically safe thing would be to move on from this episode and just hope that it fades into the woodwork. We can dismiss Reverend Wright as a crank or a demagogue, just as some have dismissed Geraldine Ferraro, in the aftermath of her recent statements, as harboring some deep-seated racial bias.

But race is an issue that I believe this nation cannot afford to ignore right now. We would be making the same mistake that Reverend Wright made in his offending sermons about America—to simplify and stereotype and amplify the negative to the point that it distorts reality.

The fact is that the comments that have been made and the issues that have surfaced over the last few weeks reflect the complexities of race in this country that we've never really worked through—a part of our union that we have yet to perfect. And if we walk away now, if we simply retreat into our respective corners, we will never be able to come together and solve challenges like health care, or education, or the need to find good jobs for every American.

Understanding this reality requires a reminder of how we arrived at this point. As William Faulkner once wrote, "The past isn't dead and buried. In fact, it isn't even past." We do not need to recite here the history of racial injustice in this country. But we do need to remind ourselves that so many of the disparities that exist in the African-American community today can be directly traced to inequalities passed on from an earlier generation that suffered under the brutal legacy of slavery and Jim Crow.

Segregated schools were, and are, inferior schools; we still haven't fixed them, fifty years after Brown v. Board of Education, and the inferior education they provided, then and now, helps explain the pervasive achievement gap between today's black and white students.

Legalized discrimination—where blacks were prevented, often through violence, from owning property, or loans were not granted to African-American business owners, or black homeowners could not access FHA mortgages, or blacks were excluded from unions, or the police force, or fire departments—meant that black families could not amass any meaningful wealth to bequeath to future generations. That history helps explain the wealth and income gap between black and white, and the concentrated pockets of poverty that persists in so many of today's urban and rural communities.

A lack of economic opportunity among black men, and the shame and frustration that came from not being able to provide for one's family, contributed to the erosion of black families—a problem that welfare policies for many years may have worsened. And the lack of basic services in so many urban black neighborhoods—parks for kids to play in, police walking the beat, regular garbage pick-up and building code enforcement—all helped create a cycle of violence, blight and neglect that continue to haunt us.

This is the reality in which Reverend Wright and other African-Americans of his generation grew up. They came of age in the late fifties and early sixties, a time when segregation was still the law of the land and opportunity was systematically constricted. What's remarkable is not how many failed in the face of discrimination, but rather how many men and women overcame the odds; how many were able to make a way out of no way for those like me who would come after them.

But for all those who scratched and clawed their way to get a piece of the American Dream, there were many who didn't make it—those who were ultimately defeated, in one way or another, by discrimination. That legacy of defeat was passed on to future generations—those young men and increasingly young women who we see standing on street corners or languishing in our prisons, without hope or prospects for the future. Even for those blacks who did make it, questions of race, and racism, continue to define their worldview in fundamental ways. For the men and women of Reverend Wright's generation, the memories of humiliation and doubt and fear have not gone away; nor has the anger and the bitterness of those years. That anger may not get expressed in public, in front of white co-workers or white friends. But it does find voice in the barbershop or around the kitchen table. At times, that anger is exploited by politicians, to gin up votes along racial lines, or to make up for a politician's own failings.

And occasionally it finds voice in the church on Sunday morning, in the pulpit and in the pews. The fact that so many people are surprised to hear that anger in some of Reverend Wright's sermons simply reminds us of the old truism that the most segregated hour in American life occurs on Sunday morning. That anger is not always productive; indeed, all too often it distracts attention from solving real problems; it keeps us from squarely facing our own complicity in our condition, and prevents the African-American community from forging the alliances it needs to bring about real change. But the anger is real; it is powerful; and to simply wish it away, to condemn it without understanding its roots, only serves to widen the chasm of misunderstanding that exists between the races.

In fact, a similar anger exists within segments of the white community. Most working- and middle-class white Americans don't feel that they have been particularly privileged by their race. Their experience is the immigrant experience—as far as they're concerned, no one's handed them anything, they've built it from scratch. They've worked hard all their lives, many times only to see their jobs shipped overseas or their pension dumped after a lifetime of labor. They are anxious about their futures, and feel their dreams slipping away; in an era of stagnant wages and global competition, opportunity comes to be seen as a zero sum game, in which your dreams come at my expense. So when they are told to bus their children to a school across town; when they hear that an African American is getting an advantage in landing a good job or a spot in a good college because of an injustice that they themselves never committed; when they're told that their fears about crime in urban neighborhoods are somehow prejudiced, resentment builds over time.

Like the anger within the black community, these resentments aren't always expressed in polite company. But they have helped shape the political landscape for at least a generation. Anger over welfare and affirmative action helped forge the Reagan Coalition. Politicians routinely exploited fears of crime for their own electoral ends. Talk show hosts and conservative commentators built entire careers unmasking bogus claims of racism while dismissing legitimate discussions of racial injustice and inequality as mere political correctness or reverse racism.

Just as black anger often proved counterproductive, so have these white resentments distracted attention from the real culprits of the middle class squeeze—a corporate culture rife with inside dealing, questionable accounting practices, and short-term greed; a Washington dominated by lobbyists and special interests; economic policies that favor the few over the many. And yet, to wish away the resentments of white Americans, to label them as misguided or even racist, without recognizing they are grounded in legitimate concerns—this too widens the racial divide, and blocks the path to understanding.

This is where we are right now. It's a racial stalemate we've been stuck in for years. Contrary to the claims of some of my critics, black and white, I have never been so naïve as to believe that we can get beyond our racial divisions in a single election cycle, or with a single candidacy—particularly a candidacy as imperfect as my own.

But I have asserted a firm conviction—a conviction rooted in my faith in God and my faith in the American people—that working together we can move beyond some of our old racial wounds, and that in fact we have no choice if we are to continue on the path of a more perfect union.

For the African-American community, that path means embracing the burdens of our past without becoming victims of our past. It means continuing to insist on a full measure of justice in every aspect of American life. But it also means binding our particular grievances—for better health care, and better schools, and better jobs—to the larger aspirations of all Americans—the white woman struggling to break the glass ceiling, the white man whose been laid off, the immigrant trying to feed his family. And it means taking full responsibility for own lives—by demanding more from our fathers, and spending more time with our children, and reading to them, and teaching them that while they may face challenges and discrimination in their own lives, they must never succumb to despair or cynicism; they must always believe that they can write their own destiny.

Ironically, this quintessentially American—and yes, conservative—notion of self-help found frequent expression in Reverend Wright's sermons. But what my former pastor too often failed to understand is that embarking on a program of self-help also requires a belief that society can change.

The profound mistake of Reverend Wright's sermons is not that he spoke about racism in our society. It's that he spoke as if our society was static; as if no progress has been made; as if this country—a country that has made it possible for one of his own members to run for the highest office in the land and build a coalition of white and black; Latino and Asian, rich and poor, young and old—is still irrevocably bound to a tragic past. But what we know—what we have seen—is that America can change. That is true genius of this nation. What we have already achieved gives us hope—the audacity to hope—for what we can and must achieve tomorrow.

In the white community, the path to a more perfect union means acknowledging that what ails the African-American community does not just exist in the minds of black people; that the legacy of discrimination—and current incidents of discrimination, while less overt than in the past—are real and must be addressed. Not just with words, but with deeds—by investing in our schools and our communities; by enforcing our civil rights laws and ensuring fairness in our criminal justice system; by providing this generation with ladders of opportunity that were unavailable for previous generations. It requires all Americans to realize that your dreams do not have to come at the expense of my dreams; that investing in the health, welfare, and education of black and brown and white children will ultimately help all of America prosper.

In the end, then, what is called for is nothing more, and nothing less, than what all the world's great religions demand—that we do unto others as we would have them do unto us. Let us be our brother's keeper, Scripture tells us. Let us be our sister's keeper. Let us find that common stake we all have in one another, and let our politics reflect that spirit as well.

For we have a choice in this country. We can accept a politics that breeds division, and conflict, and cynicism. We can tackle race only as spectacle—as we did in the OJ trial—or in the wake of tragedy, as we did in the aftermath of Katrina—or as fodder for the nightly news. We can play Reverend Wright's sermons on every channel, every day and talk about them from now until the election, and make the only question in this campaign whether or not the American people think that I somehow believe or sympathize with his most offensive words. We can pounce on some gaffe by a Hillary supporter as evidence that she's playing the race card, or we can speculate on whether white men will all flock to John McCain in the general election regardless of his policies.

We can do that.

But if we do, I can tell you that in the next election, we'll be talking about some other distraction. And then another one. And then another one. And nothing will change.

That is one option. Or, at this moment, in this election, we can come together and say, "Not this time." This time we want to talk about the crumbling schools that are stealing the future of black children and white children and Asian children and Hispanic children and Native American children. This time we want to reject the cynicism that tells us that these kids can't learn; that those kids who don't look like us are somebody else's problem. The children of America are not those kids, they are our kids, and we will not let them fall behind in a 21st century economy. Not this time.

This time we want to talk about how the lines in the Emergency Room are filled with whites and blacks and Hispanics who do not have health care; who don't have the power on their own to overcome the special interests in Washington, but who can take them on if we do it together.

This time we want to talk about the shuttered mills that once provided a decent life for men and women of every race, and the homes for sale that once belonged to Americans from every religion, every region, every walk of life. This time we want to talk about the fact that the real problem is not that someone who doesn't look like you might take your job; it's that the corporation you work for will ship it overseas for nothing more than a profit.

This time we want to talk about the men and women of every color and creed who serve together, and fight together, and bleed together under the same proud flag. We want to talk about how to bring them home from a war that never should've been authorized and never should've been waged, and we want to talk about how we'll show our patriotism by caring for them, and their families, and giving them the benefits they have earned.

I would not be running for President if I didn't believe with all my heart that this is what the vast majority of Americans want for this country. This union may never be perfect, but generation after generation has shown that it can always be perfected. And today, whenever I find myself feeling doubtful or cynical about this possibility, what gives me the most hope is the next generation—the young people whose attitudes and beliefs and openness to change have already made history in this election.

There is one story in particularly that I'd like to leave you with today— a story I told when I had the great honor of speaking on Dr. King's birthday at his home church, Ebenezer Baptist, in Atlanta.

There is a young, twenty-three year old white woman named Ashley Baia who organized for our campaign in Florence, South Carolina. She had been working to organize a mostly African-American community since the beginning of this campaign, and one day she was at a roundtable discussion where everyone went around telling their story and why they were there.

And Ashley said that when she was nine years old, her mother got cancer. And because she had to miss days of work, she was let go and lost her health care. They had to file for bankruptcy, and that's when Ashley decided that she had to do something to help her mom.

She knew that food was one of their most expensive costs, and so Ashley convinced her mother that what she really liked and really wanted to eat more than anything else was mustard and relish sandwiches. Because that was the cheapest way to eat.

She did this for a year until her mom got better, and she told everyone at the roundtable that the reason she joined our campaign was so that she could help the millions of other children in the country who want and need to help their parents too.

Now Ashley might have made a different choice. Perhaps somebody told her along the way that the source of her mother's problems were blacks who were on welfare and too lazy to work, or Hispanics who were coming into the country illegally. But she didn't. She sought out allies in her fight against injustice.

Anyway, Ashley finishes her story and then goes around the room and asks everyone else why they're supporting the campaign. They all have different stories and reasons. Many bring up a specific issue. And finally they come to this elderly black man who's been sitting there quietly the entire time. And Ashley asks him why he's there. And he does not bring up a specific issue. He does not say health care or the economy. He does not say education or the war. He does not say that he was there because of Barack Obama. He simply says to everyone in the room, "I am here because of Ashley."

"I'm here because of Ashley." By itself, that single moment of recognition between that young white girl and that old black man is not enough. It is not enough to give health care to the sick, or jobs to the jobless, or education to our children.

But it is where we start. It is where our union grows stronger. And as so many generations have come to realize over the course of the two-hundred and twenty one years since a band of patriots signed that document in Philadelphia, that is where the perfection begins.

U.S. Senator Barack Obama: Speech in Germany

Berlin, Germany

July 24, 2008

*T*hank you to the citizens of Berlin and to the people of Germany. Let me thank Chancellor Merkel and Foreign Minister Steinmeier for welcoming me earlier today. Thank you Mayor Wowereit, the Berlin Senate, the police, and most of all thank you for this welcome.

I come to Berlin as so many of my countrymen have come before. Tonight, I speak to you not as a candidate for President, but as a citizen—a proud citizen of the United States, and a fellow citizen of the world.

I know that I don't look like the Americans who've previously spoken in this great city. The journey that led me here is improbable. My mother was born in the heartland of America, but my father grew up herding goats in Kenya. His father—my grandfather—was a cook, a domestic servant to the British.

At the height of the Cold War, my father decided, like so many others in the forgotten corners of the world, that his yearning—his dream—required the freedom and opportunity promised by the West. And so he wrote letter after letter to universities all across America until somebody, somewhere answered his prayer for a better life.

That is why I'm here. And you are here because you too know that yearning. This city, of all cities, knows the dream of freedom. And you know that the only reason we stand here tonight is because men and women from both of our nations came together to work, and struggle, and sacrifice for that better life.

Ours is a partnership that truly began sixty years ago this summer, on the day when the first American plane touched down at Templehof.

On that day, much of this continent still lay in ruin. The rubble of this city had yet to be built into a wall. The Soviet shadow had swept across Eastern Europe, while in the West, America, Britain, and France took stock of their losses, and pondered how the world might be remade.

This is where the two sides met. And on the twenty-fourth of June, 1948, the Communists chose to blockade the western part of the city. They cut off food and supplies to more than two million Germans in an effort to extinguish the last flame of freedom in Berlin.

The size of our forces was no match for the much larger Soviet Army. And yet retreat would have allowed Communism to march across Europe. Where the last war had ended, another World War could have easily begun. All that stood in the way was Berlin.

And that's when the airlift began—when the largest and most unlikely rescue in history brought food and hope to the people of this city.

The odds were stacked against success. In the winter, a heavy fog filled the sky above, and many planes were forced to turn back without dropping off the needed supplies. The streets where we stand were filled with hungry families who had no comfort from the cold.

But in the darkest hours, the people of Berlin kept the flame of hope burning. The people of Berlin refused to give up. And on one fall day, hundreds of thousands of Berliners came here, to the Tiergarten, and heard the city's mayor implore the world not to give up on freedom. "There is only one possibility," he said. "For us to stand together united until this battle is won...The people of Berlin have spoken. We have done our duty, and we will keep on doing our duty. People of the world: now do your duty... People of the world, look at Berlin!"

People of the world—look at Berlin!

Look at Berlin, where Germans and Americans learned to work together and trust each other less than three years after facing each other on the field of battle.

Look at Berlin, where the determination of a people met the generosity of the Marshall Plan and created a German miracle; where a victory over tyranny gave rise to NATO, the greatest alliance ever formed to defend our common security.

Look at Berlin, where the bullet holes in the buildings and the somber stones and pillars near the Brandenburg Gate insist that we never forget our common humanity.

People of the world—look at Berlin, where a wall came down, a continent came together, and history proved that there is no challenge too great for a world that stands as one.

Sixty years after the airlift, we are called upon again. History has led us to a new crossroad, with new promise and new peril. When you, the German people, tore down that wall—a wall that divided East and West; freedom and tyranny; fear and hope—walls came tumbling down around the world. From Kiev to Cape Town, prison camps were closed, and the doors of democracy were opened. Markets opened too, and the spread of information and technology reduced barriers to opportunity and prosperity. While the 20th century taught us that we share a common destiny, the 21st has revealed a world more intertwined than at any time in human history.

The fall of the Berlin Wall brought new hope. But that very closeness has given rise to new dangers—dangers that cannot be contained within the borders of a country or by the distance of an ocean.

The terrorists of September 11th plotted in Hamburg and trained in Kandahar and Karachi before killing thousands from all over the globe on American soil.

As we speak, cars in Boston and factories in Beijing are melting the ice caps in the Arctic, shrinking coastlines in the Atlantic, and bringing drought to farms from Kansas to Kenya.

Poorly secured nuclear material in the former Soviet Union, or secrets from a scientist in Pakistan could help build a bomb that detonates in Paris. The poppies in Afghanistan become the heroin in Berlin. The poverty and violence in Somalia breeds the terror of tomorrow. The genocide in Darfur shames the conscience of us all.

In this new world, such dangerous currents have swept along faster than our efforts to contain them. That is why we cannot afford to be divided. No one nation, no matter how large or powerful, can defeat such challenges alone. None of us can deny these threats, or escape responsibility in meeting them. Yet, in the absence of Soviet tanks and a terrible wall, it has become easy to forget this truth. And if we're honest with each other, we know that sometimes, on both sides of the Atlantic, we have drifted apart, and forgotten our shared destiny.

In Europe, the view that America is part of what has gone wrong in our world, rather than a force to help make it right, has become all too common. In America, there are voices that deride and deny the importance of Europe's role in our security and our future. Both views miss the truth—that Europeans today are bearing new burdens and taking more responsibility in critical parts of the world; and that just as American bases built in the last century still help to defend the security of this continent, so does our country still sacrifice greatly for freedom around the globe.

Yes, there have been differences between America and Europe. No doubt, there will be differences in the future. But the burdens of global citizenship continue to bind us together. A change of leadership in Washington will not lift this burden. In this new century, Americans and Europeans alike will be required to do more—not less. Partnership and cooperation among nations is not a choice; it is the one way, the only way, to protect our common security and advance our common humanity.

That is why the greatest danger of all is to allow new walls to divide us from one another.

The walls between old allies on either side of the Atlantic cannot stand. The walls between the countries with the most and those with the least cannot stand. The walls between races and tribes; natives and immigrants; Christian and Muslim and Jew cannot stand. These now are the walls we must tear down.

We know they have fallen before. After centuries of strife, the people of Europe have formed a Union of promise and prosperity. Here, at the base of a column built to mark victory in war, we meet in the center of a Europe at peace. Not only have walls come down in Berlin, but they have come down in Belfast, where Protestant and Catholic found a way to live together; in the Balkans, where our Atlantic alliance ended wars and brought savage war criminals to justice; and in South Africa, where the struggle of a courageous people defeated apartheid.

So history reminds us that walls can be torn down. But the task is never easy. True partnership and true progress requires constant work and sustained sacrifice. They require sharing the burdens of development and diplomacy; of progress and peace. They require allies who will listen to each other, learn from each other and, most of all, trust each other.

That is why America cannot turn inward. That is why Europe cannot turn inward. America has no better partner than Europe. Now is the time to build new bridges across the globe as strong as the one that bound us across the Atlantic. Now is the time to join together, through constant cooperation, strong institutions, shared sacrifice, and a global commitment to progress, to meet the challenges of the 21st century. It was this spirit that led airlift planes to appear in the sky above our heads, and people to assemble where we stand today. And this is the moment when our nations—and all nations—must summon that spirit anew.

This is the moment when we must defeat terror and dry up the well of extremism that supports it. This threat is real and we cannot shrink from our responsibility to combat it. If we could create NATO to face down the Soviet Union, we can join in a new and global partnership to dismantle the networks that have struck in Madrid and Amman; in London and Bali; in Washington and New York. If we could win a battle of ideas against the communists, we can stand with the vast majority of Muslims who reject the extremism that leads to hate instead of hope.

This is the moment when we must renew our resolve to rout the terrorists who threaten our security in Afghanistan, and the traffickers who sell drugs on your streets. No one welcomes war. I recognize the enormous difficulties in Afghanistan. But my country and yours have a stake in seeing that NATO's first mission beyond Europe's borders is a success. For the people of Afghanistan, and for our shared security, the work must be done. America cannot do this alone. The Afghan people need our troops and your troops; our support and your support to defeat the Taliban and al Qaeda, to develop their economy, and to help them rebuild their nation. We have too much at stake to turn back now.

This is the moment when we must renew the goal of a world without nuclear weapons. The two superpowers that faced each other across the wall of this city came too close too often to destroying all we have built and all that we love. With that wall gone, we need not stand idly by and watch the further spread of the deadly atom. It is time to secure all loose nuclear materials; to stop the spread of nuclear weapons; and to reduce the arsenals from another era. This is the moment to begin the work of seeking the peace of a world without nuclear weapons.

This is the moment when every nation in Europe must have the chance to choose its own tomorrow free from the shadows of yesterday. In this century, we need a strong European Union that deepens the security and prosperity of this continent, while extending a hand abroad. In this century—in this city of all cities—we must reject the Cold War mind-set of the past, and resolve to work with Russia when we can, to stand up for our values when we must, and to seek a partnership that extends across this entire continent.

This is the moment when we must build on the wealth that open markets have created, and share its benefits more equitably. Trade has been a cornerstone of our growth and global development. But we will not be able to sustain this growth if it favors the few, and not the many. Together, we must forge trade that truly rewards the work that creates wealth, with meaningful protections for our people and our planet. This is the moment for trade that is free and fair for all.

This is the moment we must help answer the call for a new dawn in the Middle East. My country must stand with yours and with Europe in sending a direct message to Iran that it must abandon its nuclear ambitions. We must support the Lebanese who have marched and bled for democracy, and the Israelis and Palestinians who seek a secure and lasting peace. And despite past differences, this is the moment when the world should support the millions of Iraqis who seek to rebuild their lives, even as we pass responsibility to the Iraqi government and finally bring this war to a close.

This is the moment when we must come together to save this planet. Let us resolve that we will not leave our children a world where the oceans rise and famine spreads and terrible storms devastate our lands. Let us resolve that all nations—including my own—will act with the same seriousness of purpose as has your nation, and reduce the carbon we send into our atmosphere. This is the moment to give our children back their future. This is the moment to stand as one.

And this is the moment when we must give hope to those left behind in a globalized world. We must remember that the Cold War born in this city was not a battle for land or treasure. Sixty years ago, the planes that flew over Berlin did not drop bombs; instead they delivered food, and coal, and candy to grateful children. And in that show of solidarity, those pilots won more than a military victory. They won hearts and minds; love and loyalty and trust—not just from the people in this city, but from all those who heard the story of what they did here.

Now the world will watch and remember what we do here—what we do with this moment. Will we extend our hand to the people in the forgotten corners of this world who yearn for lives marked by dignity and opportunity; by security and justice? Will we lift the child in Bangladesh from poverty, shelter the refugee in Chad, and banish the scourge of AIDS in our time?

Will we stand for the human rights of the dissident in Burma, the blogger in Iran, or the voter in Zimbabwe? Will we give meaning to the words "never again" in Darfur?

Will we acknowledge that there is no more powerful example than the one each of our nations projects to the world? Will we reject torture and stand for the rule of law? Will we welcome immigrants from different lands, and shun discrimination against those who don't look like us or worship like we do, and keep the promise of equality and opportunity for all of our people?

People of Berlin—people of the world—this is our moment. This is our time.

I know my country has not perfected itself. At times, we've struggled to keep the promise of liberty and equality for all of our people. We've made our share of mistakes, and there are times when our actions around the world have not lived up to our best intentions.

But I also know how much I love America. I know that for more than two centuries, we have strived—at great cost and great sacrifice—to form a more perfect union; to seek, with other nations, a more hopeful world. Our allegiance has never been to any particular tribe or kingdom—indeed, every language is spoken in our country; every culture has left its imprint on ours; every point of view is expressed in our public squares. What has always united us—what has always driven our people; what drew my father to America's shores—is a set of ideals that speak to aspirations shared by all people: that we can live free from fear and free from want; that we can speak our minds and assemble with whomever we choose and worship as we please.

These are the aspirations that joined the fates of all nations in this city. These aspirations are bigger than anything that drives us apart. It is because of these aspirations that the airlift began. It is because of these aspirations that all free people—everywhere—became citizens of Berlin. It is in pursuit of these aspirations that a new generation—our generation—must make our mark on the world.

People of Berlin—and people of the world—the scale of our challenge is great. The road ahead will be long. But I come before you to say that we are heirs to a struggle for freedom. We are a people of improbable hope. With an eye toward the future, with resolve in our hearts, let us remember this history, and answer our destiny, and remake the world once again.

Context

⚜

U.S. Senator Hillary Clinton: Speech at the Democratic National Convention

Denver, CO

August 26, 2008

I am honored to be here tonight. A proud mother. A proud Democrat. A proud American. And a proud supporter of Barack Obama.

My friends, it is time to take back the country we love.

Whether you voted for me, or voted for Barack, the time is now to unite as a single party with a single purpose. We are on the same team, and none of us can sit on the sidelines.

This is a fight for the future. And it's a fight we must win.

I haven't spent the past 35 years in the trenches advocating for children, campaigning for universal health care, helping parents balance work and family, and fighting for women's rights at home and around the world ... to see another Republican in the White House squander the promise of our country and the hopes of our people.

And you haven't worked so hard over the last 18 months, or endured the last eight years, to suffer through more failed leadership.

No way. No how. No McCain.

Barack Obama is my candidate. And he must be our President.

Tonight we need to remember what a Presidential election is really about. When the polls have closed, and the ads are finally off the air, it comes down to you—the American people, your lives, and your children's futures.

For me, it's been a privilege to meet you in your homes, your workplaces, and your communities. Your stories reminded me everyday that America's greatness is bound up in the lives of the American people—your hard work, your devotion to duty, your love for your children, and your determination to keep going, often in the face of enormous obstacles.

You taught me so much, you made me laugh, and ... you even made me cry. You allowed me to become part of your lives. And you became part of mine.

I will always remember the single mom who had adopted two kids with autism, didn't have health insurance and discovered she had cancer. But she greeted me with her bald head painted with my name on it and asked me to fight for health care.

I will always remember the young man in a Marine Corps t-shirt who waited months for medical care and said to me: "Take care of my buddies; a lot of them are still over there....and then will you please help take care of me?"

I will always remember the boy who told me his mom worked for the minimum wage and that her employer had cut her hours. He said he just didn't know what his family was going to do.

I will always be grateful to everyone from all fifty states, Puerto Rico and the territories, who joined our campaign on behalf of all those people left out and left behind by the Bush Administrtation.

To my supporters, my champions—my sisterhood of the traveling pantsuits – from the bottom of my heart: Thank you.

You never gave in. You never gave up. And together we made history.

Along the way, America lost two great Democratic champions who would have been here with us tonight. One of our finest young leaders, Arkansas Democratic Party Chair, Bill Gwatney, who believed with all his heart that America and the South could be and should be Democratic from top to bottom.

And Congresswoman Stephanie Tubbs Jones, a dear friend to many of us, a loving mother and courageous leader who never gave up her quest to make America fairer and smarter, stronger and better. Steadfast in her beliefs, a fighter of uncommon grace, she was an inspiration to me and to us all.

Our heart goes out to Stephanie's son, Mervyn, Jr, and Bill's wife, Rebecca, who traveled to Denver to join us at our convention.

Bill and Stephanie knew that after eight years of George Bush, people are hurting at home, and our standing has eroded around the world. We have a lot of work ahead.

Jobs lost, houses gone, falling wages, rising prices. The Supreme Court in a right-wing headlock and our government in partisan gridlock. The biggest deficit in our nation's history. Money borrowed from the Chinese to buy oil from the Saudis.

Putin and Georgia, Iraq and Iran.

I ran for President to renew the promise of America. To rebuild the middle class and sustain the American Dream, to provide the opportunity to work hard and have that work rewarded, to save for college, a home and retirement, to afford the gas and groceries and still have a little left over each month.

To promote a clean energy economy that will create millions of green collar jobs.

To create a health care system that is universal, high quality, and affordable so that parents no longer have to choose between care for themselves or their children or be stuck in dead end jobs simply to keep their insurance.

To create a world class education system and make college affordable again.

To fight for an America defined by deep and meaningful equality— from civil rights to labor rights, from women's rights to gay rights, from ending discrimination to promoting unionization to providing help for the most important job there is: caring for our families. To help every child live up to his or her God-given potential.

To make America once again a nation of immigrants and a nation of laws.

To bring fiscal sanity back to Washington and make our government an instrument of the public good, not of private plunder.

To restore America's standing in the world, to end the war in Iraq, bring our troops home and honor their service by caring for our veterans.

And to join with our allies to confront our shared challenges, f rom poverty and genocide to terrorism and global warming.

Most of all, I ran to stand up for all those who have been invisible to their government for eight long years.

Those are the reasons I ran for President. Those are the reasons I support Barack Obama. And those are the reasons you should too.

I want you to ask yourselves: Were you in this campaign just for me? Or were you in it for that young Marine and others like him? Were you in it for that mom struggling with cancer while raising her kids? Were you in it for that boy and his mom surviving on the minimum wage? Were you in it for all the people in this country who feel invisible?

We need leaders once again who can tap in-to that special blend of American confidence and optimism that has enabled generations before us to meet our toughest challenges. Leaders who can help us show ourselves and the world that with our ingenuity, creativity, and innovative spirit, there are no limits to what is possible in America.

This won't be easy. Progress never is. But it will be impossible if we don't fight to put a Democrat in the White House.

We need to elect Barack Obama because we need a President who understands that America can't compete in a global economy by padding the pockets of energy speculators, while ignoring the workers whose jobs have been shipped overseas. We need a President who understands that we can't solve the problems of global warming by giving windfall profits to the oil companies while ignoring opportunities to invest in new technologies that will build a green economy.

We need a President who understands that the genius of America has always depended on the strength and vitality of the middle class.

Barack Obama began his career fighting for workers displaced by the global economy. He built his campaign on a fundamental belief that change in this country must start from the ground up, not the top down. He knows government must be about "We the people" not "We the favored few."

And when Barack Obama is in the White House, he'll revitalize our economy, defend the working people of America, and meet the global challenges of our time. Democrats know how to do this. As I recall, President Clinton and the Democrats did it before. And President Obama and the Democrats will do it again.

He'll transform our energy agenda by creating millions of green jobs and building a new, clean energy future. He'll make sure that middle class families get the tax relief they deserve. And I can't wait to watch Barack Obama sign a health care plan in-to law that covers every single American.

Barack Obama will end the war in Iraq responsibly and bring our troops home – a first step to repairing our alliances around the world.

And he will have with him a terrific partner in Michelle Obama. Anyone who saw Michelle's speech last night knows she will be a great First Lady for America.

Americans are also fortunate that Joe Biden will be at Barack Obama's side. He is a strong leader and a good man. He understands both the economic stresses here at home and the strategic challenges abroad. He is pragmatic, tough, and wise. And, of course, Joe will be supported by his wonderful wife, Jill.

They will be a great team for our country.

Now, John McCain is my colleague and my friend.

He has served our country with honor and courage.

But we don't need four more years ... of the last eight years.

More economic stagnation ...and less affordable health care.

More high gas prices ...and less alternative energy.

More jobs getting shipped overseas ...and fewer jobs created here.

More skyrocketing debt ...home foreclosures ...and mounting bills that are crushing our middle class families.

More war ... less diplomacy.

More of a government where the privileged come first …and everyone else comes last.

John McCain says the economy is fundamentally sound. John Mc-Cain doesn't think that 47 million people without health insurance is a crisis. John McCain wants to privatize Social Security. And in 2008, he still thinks it's okay when women don't earn equal pay for equal work.

With an agenda like that, it makes sense that George Bush and John McCain will be together next week in the Twin Cities. Because these days they're awfully hard to tell apart.

America is still around after 232 years because we have risen to the challenge of every new time, changing to be faithful to our values of equal opportunity for all and the common good.

And I know what that can mean for every man, woman, and child in America. I'm a United States Senator because in 1848 a group of courageous women and a few brave men gathered in Seneca Falls, New York, many traveling for days and nights, to participate in the first convention on women's rights in our history.

And so dawned a struggle for the right to vote that would last 72 years, handed down by mother to daughter to granddaughter – and a few sons and grandsons along the way.

These women and men looked in-to their daughters' eyes, imagined a fairer and freer world, and found the strength to fight. To rally and picket. To endure ridicule and harassment. To brave violence and jail.

And after so many decades – 88 years ago on this very day – the 19th amendment guaranteeing women the right to vote would be forever enshrined in our Constitution.

My mother was born before women could vote. But in this election my daughter got to vote for her mother for President.

This is the story of America. Of women and men who defy the odds and never give up.

How do we give this country back to them?

By following the example of a brave New Yorker , a woman who risked her life to shepherd slaves along the Underground Railroad.

And on that path to freedom, Harriett Tubman had one piece of advice. If you hear the dogs, keep going.

If you see the torches in the woods, keep going.

If they're shouting after you, keep going.

Don't ever stop. Keep going.

If you want a taste of freedom, keep going.

Even in the darkest of moments, ordinary Americans have found the faith to keep going.

I've seen it in you. I've seen it in our teachers and firefighters, nurses and police officers, small business owners and union workers, the men and women of our military – you always keep going.

We are Americans. We're not big on quitting.

But remember, before we can keep going, we have to get going by electing Barack Obama president.

We don't have a moment to lose or a vote to spare.

Nothing less than the fate of our nation and the future of our children hang in the balance.

I want you to think about your children and grandchildren come election day. And think about the choices your parents and grandparents made that had such a big impact on your life and on the life of our nation.

We've got to ensure that the choice we make in this election honors the sacrifices of all who came before us, and will fill the lives of our children with possibility and hope.

That is our duty, to build that bright future, and to teach our children that in America there is no chasm too deep, no barrier too great – and no ceiling too high – for all who work hard, never back down, always keep going, have faith in God, in our country, and in each other.

Thank you so much. God bless America and Godspeed to you all.

U.S. Senator Barack Obama:

"The American Promise"

(Accepting the Democratic Nomination at the Democratic National Convention)

Denver, CO

August 28, 2008

To Chairman Dean and my great friend Dick Durbin; and to all my fellow citizens of this great nation;

With profound gratitude and great humility, I accept your nomination for the presidency of the United States.

Let me express my thanks to the historic slate of candidates who accompanied me on this journey, and especially the one who traveled the farthest—a champion for working Americans and an inspiration to my daughters and to yours—Hillary Rodham Clinton. To President Clinton, who last night made the case for change as only he can make it; to Ted Kennedy, who embodies the spirit of service; and to the next Vice President of the United States, Joe Biden, I thank you. I am grateful to finish this journey with one of the finest statesmen of our time, a man at ease with everyone from world leaders to the conductors on the Amtrak train he still takes home every night.

To the love of my life, our next First Lady, Michelle Obama, and to Sasha and Malia—I love you so much, and I'm so proud of all of you.

Four years ago, I stood before you and told you my story—of the brief union between a young man from Kenya and a young woman from Kansas who weren't well-off or well-known, but shared a belief that in America, their son could achieve whatever he put his mind to.

It is that promise that has always set this country apart—that through hard work and sacrifice, each of us can pursue our individual dreams but still come together as one American family, to ensure that the next generation can pursue their dreams as well.

That's why I stand here tonight. Because for two hundred and thirty two years, at each moment when that promise was in jeopardy, ordinary men and women—students and soldiers, farmers and teachers, nurses and janitors—found the courage to keep it alive.

We meet at one of those defining moments—a moment when our nation is at war, our economy is in turmoil, and the American promise has been threatened once more.

Tonight, more Americans are out of work and more are working harder for less. More of you have lost your homes and even more are watching your home values plummet. More of you have cars you can't afford to drive, credit card bills you can't afford to pay, and tuition that's beyond your reach.

These challenges are not all of government's making. But the failure to respond is a direct result of a broken politics in Washington and the failed policies of George W. Bush.

America, we are better than these last eight years. We are a better country than this.

This country is more decent than one where a woman in Ohio, on the brink of retirement, finds herself one illness away from disaster after a lifetime of hard work.

This country is more generous than one where a man in Indiana has to pack up the equipment he's worked on for twenty years and watch it shipped off to China, and then chokes up as he explains how he felt like a failure when he went home to tell his family the news.

We are more compassionate than a government that lets veterans sleep on our streets and families slide into poverty; that sits on its hands while a major American city drowns before our eyes.

Tonight, I say to the American people, to Democrats and Republicans and Independents across this great land—enough! This moment—this election—is our chance to keep, in the 21st century, the American promise alive. Because next week, in Minnesota, the same party that brought you two terms of George Bush and Dick Cheney will ask this country for a third. And we are here because we love this country too much to let the next four years look like the last eight. On November 4th, we must stand up and say: "Eight is enough."

Now let there be no doubt. The Republican nominee, John McCain, has worn the uniform of our country with bravery and distinction, and for that we owe him our gratitude and respect. And next week, we'll also hear about those occasions when he's broken with his party as evidence that he can deliver the change that we need.

But the record's clear: John McCain has voted with George Bush ninety percent of the time. Senator McCain likes to talk about judgment, but really, what does it say about your judgment when you think George Bush has been right more than ninety percent of the time? I don't know about you, but I'm not ready to take a ten percent chance on change.

The truth is, on issue after issue that would make a difference in your lives—on health care and education and the economy—Senator McCain has been anything but independent. He said that our economy has made "great progress" under this President. He said that the fundamentals of the economy are strong. And when one of his chief advisors—the man who wrote his economic plan—was talking about the anxiety Americans are feeling, he said that we were just suffering from a "mental recession," and that we've become, and I quote, "a nation of whiners." A nation of whiners? Tell that to the proud auto workers at a Michigan plant who, after they found out it was closing, kept showing up every day and working as hard as ever, because they knew there were people who counted on the brakes that they made. Tell that to the military families who shoulder their burdens silently as they watch their loved ones leave for their third or fourth or fifth tour of duty. These are not whiners. They work hard and give back and keep going without complaint. These are the Americans that I know.

Now, I don't believe that Senator McCain doesn't care what's going on in the lives of Americans. I just think he doesn't know. Why else would he define middle-class as someone making under five million dollars a year? How else could he propose hundreds of billions in tax breaks for big corporations and oil companies but not one penny of tax relief to more than one hundred million Americans? How else could he offer a health care plan that would actually tax people's benefits, or an education plan that would do nothing to help families pay for college, or a plan that would privatize Social Security and gamble your retirement?

It's not because John McCain doesn't care. It's because John McCain doesn't get it.

For over two decades, he's subscribed to that old, discredited Republican philosophy—give more and more to those with the most and hope that prosperity trickles down to everyone else. In Washington, they call this the Ownership Society, but what it really means is—you're on your own. Out of work? Tough luck. No health care? The market will fix it. Born into poverty? Pull yourself up by your own bootstraps—even if you don't have boots. You're on your own.

Well it's time for them to own their failure. It's time for us to change America.

You see, we Democrats have a very different measure of what constitutes progress in this country.

We measure progress by how many people can find a job that pays the mortgage; whether you can put a little extra money away at the end of each month so you can someday watch your child receive her college diploma. We measure progress in the 23 million new jobs that were created when

Bill Clinton was President—when the average American family saw its income go up $7,500 instead of down $2,000 like it has under George Bush.

We measure the strength of our economy not by the number of billionaires we have or the profits of the Fortune 500, but by whether someone with a good idea can take a risk and start a new business, or whether the waitress who lives on tips can take a day off to look after a sick kid without losing her job—an economy that honors the dignity of work.

The fundamentals we use to measure economic strength are whether we are living up to that fundamental promise that has made this country great—a promise that is the only reason I am standing here tonight.

Because in the faces of those young veterans who come back from Iraq and Afghanistan, I see my grandfather, who signed up after Pearl Harbor, marched in Patton's Army, and was rewarded by a grateful nation with the chance to go to college on the GI Bill.

In the face of that young student who sleeps just three hours before working the night shift, I think about my mom, who raised my sister and me on her own while she worked and earned her degree; who once turned to food stamps but was still able to send us to the best schools in the country with the help of student loans and scholarships.

When I listen to another worker tell me that his factory has shut down, I remember all those men and women on the South Side of Chicago who I stood by and fought for two decades ago after the local steel plant closed.

And when I hear a woman talk about the difficulties of starting her own business, I think about my grandmother, who worked her way up from the secretarial pool to middle-management, despite years of being passed over for promotions because she was a woman. She's the one who taught me about hard work. She's the one who put off buying a new car or a new dress for herself so that I could have a better life. She poured everything she had into me. And although she can no longer travel, I know that she's watching tonight, and that tonight is her night as well.

I don't know what kind of lives John McCain thinks that celebrities lead, but this has been mine. These are my heroes. Theirs are the stories that shaped me. And it is on their behalf that I intend to win this election and keep our promise alive as President of the United States.

What is that promise?

It's a promise that says each of us has the freedom to make of our own lives what we will, but that we also have the obligation to treat each other with dignity and respect.

It's a promise that says the market should reward drive and innovation and generate growth, but that businesses should live up to their responsibilities to create American jobs, look out for American workers, and play by the rules of the road.

Ours is a promise that says government cannot solve all our problems, but what it should do is that which we cannot do for ourselves—protect us from harm and provide every child a decent education; keep our water clean and our toys safe; invest in new schools and new roads and new science and technology.

Our government should work for us, not against us. It should help us, not hurt us. It should ensure opportunity not just for those with the most money and influence, but for every American who's willing to work.

That's the promise of America—the idea that we are responsible for ourselves, but that we also rise or fall as one nation; the fundamental belief that I am my brother's keeper; I am my sister's keeper.

That's the promise we need to keep. That's the change we need right now. So let me spell out exactly what that change would mean if I am President.

Change means a tax code that doesn't reward the lobbyists who wrote it, but the American workers and small businesses who deserve it.

Unlike John McCain, I will stop giving tax breaks to corporations that ship jobs overseas, and I will start giving them to companies that create good jobs right here in America.

I will eliminate capital gains taxes for the small businesses and the start-ups that will create the high-wage, high-tech jobs of tomorrow.

I will cut taxes—cut taxes—for 95% of all working families. Because in an economy like this, the last thing we should do is raise taxes on the middle-class.

And for the sake of our economy, our security, and the future of our planet, I will set a clear goal as President: in ten years, we will finally end our dependence on oil from the Middle East.

Washington's been talking about our oil addiction for the last thirty years, and John McCain has been there for twenty-six of them. In that time, he's said no to higher fuel-efficiency standards for cars, no to investments in renewable energy, no to renewable fuels. And today, we import triple the amount of oil as the day that Senator McCain took office.

Now is the time to end this addiction, and to understand that drilling is a stop-gap measure, not a long-term solution. Not even close.

As President, I will tap our natural gas reserves, invest in clean coal technology, and find ways to safely harness nuclear power. I'll help our auto companies re-tool, so that the fuel-efficient cars of the future are built right here in America. I'll make it easier for the American people to afford these new cars. And I'll invest 150 billion dollars over the next decade in affordable, renewable sources of energy—wind power and solar power and the next generation of biofuels; an investment that will lead to new industries and five million new jobs that pay well and can't ever be outsourced.

America, now is not the time for small plans.

Now is the time to finally meet our moral obligation to provide every child a world-class education, because it will take nothing less to compete in the global economy. Michelle and I are only here tonight because we were given a chance at an education. And I will not settle for an America where some kids don't have that chance. I'll invest in early childhood education. I'll recruit an army of new teachers, and pay them higher salaries and give them more support. And in exchange, I'll ask for higher standards and more accountability. And we will keep our promise to every young American—if you commit to serving your community or your country, we will make sure you can afford a college education.

Now is the time to finally keep the promise of affordable, accessible health care for every single American. If you have health care, my plan will lower your premiums. If you don't, you'll be able to get the same kind of coverage that members of Congress give themselves. And as someone who watched my mother argue with insurance companies while she lay in bed dying of cancer, I will make certain those companies stop discriminating against those who are sick and need care the most.

Now is the time to help families with paid sick days and better family leave, because nobody in America should have to choose between keeping their jobs and caring for a sick child or ailing parent.

Now is the time to change our bankruptcy laws, so that your pensions are protected ahead of CEO bonuses; and the time to protect Social Security for future generations.

And now is the time to keep the promise of equal pay for an equal day's work, because I want my daughters to have exactly the same opportunities as your sons.

Now, many of these plans will cost money, which is why I've laid out how I'll pay for every dime—by closing corporate loopholes and tax havens that don't help America grow. But I will also go through the federal budget, line by line, eliminating programs that no longer work and making the ones we do need work better and cost less—because we cannot meet twenty-first century challenges with a twentieth century bureaucracy.

And Democrats, we must also admit that fulfilling America's promise will require more than just money. It will require a renewed sense of responsibility from each of us to recover what John F. Kennedy called our "intellectual and moral strength." Yes, government must lead on energy independence, but each of us must do our part to make our homes and businesses more efficient. Yes, we must provide more ladders to success for young men who fall into lives of crime and despair. But we must also admit that programs alone can't replace parents; that government can't turn off the television and make a child do her homework; that fathers must take more responsibility for providing the love and guidance their children need.

Individual responsibility and mutual responsibility—that's the essence of America's promise.

And just as we keep our keep our promise to the next generation here at home, so must we keep America's promise abroad. If John McCain wants to have a debate about who has the temperament, and judgment, to serve as the next Commander-in-Chief, that's a debate I'm ready to have.

For while Senator McCain was turning his sights to Iraq just days after 9/11, I stood up and opposed this war, knowing that it would distract us from the real threats we face. When John McCain said we could just "muddle through" in Afghanistan, I argued for more resources and more troops to finish the fight against the terrorists who actually attacked us on 9/11, and made clear that we must take out Osama bin Laden and his lieutenants if we have them in our sights. John McCain likes to say that he'll follow bin Laden to the Gates of Hell—but he won't even go to the cave where he lives.

And today, as my call for a time frame to remove our troops from Iraq has been echoed by the Iraqi government and even the Bush Administration, even after we learned that Iraq has a $79 billion surplus while we're wallowing in deficits, John McCain stands alone in his stubborn refusal to end a misguided war.

That's not the judgment we need. That won't keep America safe. We need a President who can face the threats of the future, not keep grasping at the ideas of the past.

You don't defeat a terrorist network that operates in eighty countries by occupying Iraq. You don't protect Israel and deter Iran just by talking tough in Washington. You can't truly stand up for Georgia when you've strained our oldest alliances. If John McCain wants to follow George Bush with more tough talk and bad strategy, that is his choice—but it is not the change we need.

We are the party of Roosevelt. We are the party of Kennedy. So don't tell me that Democrats won't defend this country. Don't tell me that Democrats won't keep us safe. The Bush-McCain foreign policy has squandered the legacy that generations of Americans—Democrats and Republicans—have built, and we are here to restore that legacy.

As Commander-in-Chief, I will never hesitate to defend this nation, but I will only send our troops into harm's way with a clear mission and a sacred commitment to give them the equipment they need in battle and the care and benefits they deserve when they come home.

I will end this war in Iraq responsibly, and finish the fight against al Qaeda and the Taliban in Afghanistan. I will rebuild our military to meet future conflicts. But I will also renew the tough, direct diplomacy that can prevent Iran from obtaining nuclear weapons and curb Russian aggression. I will build new partnerships to defeat the threats of the 21st century: terrorism and nuclear proliferation; poverty and genocide; climate change and disease. And I will restore our moral standing, so that America is once again that last, best hope for all who are called to the cause of freedom, who long for lives of peace, and who yearn for a better future.

These are the policies I will pursue. And in the weeks ahead, I look forward to debating them with John McCain.

But what I will not do is suggest that the Senator takes his positions for political purposes. Because one of the things that we have to change in our politics is the idea that people cannot disagree without challenging each other's character and patriotism.

The times are too serious, the stakes are too high for this same partisan playbook. So let us agree that patriotism has no party. I love this country, and so do you, and so does John McCain. The men and women who serve in our battlefields may be Democrats and Republicans and Independents, but they have fought together and bled together and some died together under the same proud flag. They have not served a Red America or a Blue America—they have served the United States of America.

So I've got news for you, John McCain. We all put our country first.

America, our work will not be easy. The challenges we face require tough choices, and Democrats as well as Republicans will need to cast off the worn-out ideas and politics of the past. For part of what has been lost these past eight years can't just be measured by lost wages or bigger trade deficits. What has also been lost is our sense of common purpose—our sense of higher purpose. And that's what we have to restore.

We may not agree on abortion, but surely we can agree on reducing the number of unwanted pregnancies in this country. The reality of gun ownership may be different for hunters in rural Ohio than for those plagued by gang-violence in Cleveland, but don't tell me we can't uphold the Second Amendment while keeping AK-47s out of the hands of criminals. I know there are differences on same-sex marriage, but surely we can agree that our gay and lesbian brothers and sisters deserve to visit the person they love in the hospital and to live lives free of discrimination. Passions fly on immigration, but I don't know anyone who benefits when a mother is separated from her infant child or an employer undercuts American wages by hiring illegal workers. This too is part of America's promise—the promise of a democracy where we can find the strength and grace to bridge divides and unite in common effort.

I know there are those who dismiss such beliefs as happy talk. They claim that our insistence on something larger, something firmer and more honest in our public life is just a Trojan Horse for higher taxes and the abandonment of traditional values. And that's to be expected. Because if you don't have any fresh ideas, then you use stale tactics to scare the voters. If you don't have a record to run on, then you paint your opponent as someone people should run from.

You make a big election about small things.

And you know what—it's worked before. Because it feeds into the cynicism we all have about government. When Washington doesn't work, all its promises seem empty. If your hopes have been dashed again and again, then it's best to stop hoping, and settle for what you already know.

I get it. I realize that I am not the likeliest candidate for this office. I don't fit the typical pedigree, and I haven't spent my career in the halls of Washington.

But I stand before you tonight because all across America something is stirring. What the nay-sayers don't understand is that this election has never been about me. It's been about you.

For eighteen long months, you have stood up, one by one, and said enough to the politics of the past. You understand that in this election, the greatest risk we can take is to try the same old politics with the same old players and expect a different result. You have shown what history teaches us—that at defining moments like this one, the change we need doesn't come from Washington. Change comes to Washington. Change happens because the American people demand it—because they rise up and insist on new ideas and new leadership, a new politics for a new time.

America, this is one of those moments.

I believe that as hard as it will be, the change we need is coming. Because I've seen it. Because I've lived it. I've seen it in Illinois, when we provided health care to more children and moved more families from welfare to work. I've seen it in Washington, when we worked across party lines to open up government and hold lobbyists more accountable, to give better care for our veterans and keep nuclear weapons out of terrorist hands.

And I've seen it in this campaign. In the young people who voted for the first time, and in those who got involved again after a very long time. In the Republicans who never thought they'd pick up a Democratic ballot, but did. I've seen it in the workers who would rather cut their hours back a day than see their friends lose their jobs, in the soldiers who re-enlist after losing a limb, in the good neighbors who take a stranger in when a hurricane strikes and the floodwaters rise.

This country of ours has more wealth than any nation, but that's not what makes us rich. We have the most powerful military on Earth, but that's not what makes us strong. Our universities and our culture are the envy of the world, but that's not what keeps the world coming to our shores.

Instead, it is that American spirit—that American promise—that pushes us forward even when the path is uncertain; that binds us together in spite of our differences; that makes us fix our eye not on what is seen, but what is unseen, that better place around the bend.

That promise is our greatest inheritance. It's a promise I make to my daughters when I tuck them in at night, and a promise that you make to yours—a promise that has led immigrants to cross oceans and pioneers to travel west; a promise that led workers to picket lines, and women to reach for the ballot.

And it is that promise that forty five years ago today, brought Americans from every corner of this land to stand together on a Mall in Washington, before Lincoln's Memorial, and hear a young preacher from Georgia speak of his dream.

The men and women who gathered there could've heard many things. They could've heard words of anger and discord. They could've been told to succumb to the fear and frustration of so many dreams deferred.

But what the people heard instead—people of every creed and color, from every walk of life—is that in America, our destiny is inextricably linked. That together, our dreams can be one.

"We cannot walk alone," the preacher cried. "And as we walk, we must make the pledge that we shall always march ahead. We cannot turn back."

America, we cannot turn back. Not with so much work to be done. Not with so many children to educate, and so many veterans to care for. Not with an economy to fix and cities to rebuild and farms to save. Not with so many families to protect and so many lives to mend. America, we cannot turn back. We cannot walk alone. At this moment, in this election, we must pledge once more to march into the future. Let us keep that promise—that American promise—and in the words of Scripture hold firmly, without wavering, to the hope that we confess.

Thank you, God Bless you, and God Bless the United States of America.

Context

❦

U.S. Senator John McCain: Concession Speech

Phoenix, AZ

November 4, 2008

hank you. Thank you, my friends. Thank you for coming here on this beautiful Arizona evening.

My friends, we have—we have come to the end of a long journey. The American people have spoken, and they have spoken clearly.

A little while ago, I had the honor of calling Senator Barack Obama to congratulate him.

Please (following booing by the crowd).

To congratulate him on being elected the next president of the country that we both love.

In a contest as long and difficult as this campaign has been, his success alone commands my respect for his ability and perseverance. But that he managed to do so by inspiring the hopes of so many millions of Americans who had once wrongly believed that they had little at stake or little influence in the election of an American president is something I deeply admire and commend him for achieving.

This is an historic election, and I recognize the special significance it has for African-Americans and for the special pride that must be theirs tonight.

I've always believed that America offers opportunities to all who have the industry and will to seize it. Senator Obama believes that, too.

But we both recognize that, though we have come a long way from the old injustices that once stained our nation's reputation and denied some Americans the full blessings of American citizenship, the memory of them still had the power to wound.

A century ago, President Theodore Roosevelt's invitation of Booker T. Washington to dine at the White House was taken as an outrage in many quarters.

America today is a world away from the cruel and frightful bigotry of that time. There is no better evidence of this than the election of an African-American to the presidency of the United States.

Let there be no reason now ... Let there be no reason now for any American to fail to cherish their citizenship in this, the greatest nation on Earth.

Senator Obama has achieved a great thing for himself and for his country. I applaud him for it, and offer him my sincere sympathy that his beloved grandmother did not live to see this day. Though our faith assures us she is at rest in the presence of her creator and so very proud of the good man she helped raise.

Senator Obama and I have had and argued our differences, and he has prevailed. No doubt many of those differences remain.

These are difficult times for our country. And I pledge to him tonight to do all in my power to help him lead us through the many challenges we face.

I urge all Americans ... I urge all Americans who supported me to join me in not just congratulating him, but offering our next president our good will and earnest effort to find ways to come together to find the necessary compromises to bridge our differences and help restore our prosperity, defend our security in a dangerous world, and leave our children and grandchildren a stronger, better country than we inherited.

Whatever our differences, we are fellow Americans. And please believe me when I say no association has ever meant more to me than that.

It is natural. It's natural, tonight, to feel some disappointment. But tomorrow, we must move beyond it and work together to get our country moving again.

We fought—we fought as hard as we could. And though we feel short, the failure is mine, not yours.

I am so deeply grateful to all of you for the great honor of your support and for all you have done for me. I wish the outcome had been different, my friends.

The road was a difficult one from the outset, but your support and friendship never wavered. I cannot adequately express how deeply indebted I am to you.

I'm especially grateful to my wife, Cindy, my children, my dear mother ... my dear mother and all my family, and to the many old and dear friends who have stood by my side through the many ups and downs of this long campaign.

I have always been a fortunate man, and never more so for the love and encouragement you have given me.

You know, campaigns are often harder on a candidate's family than on the candidate, and that's been true in this campaign.

All I can offer in compensation is my love and gratitude and the promise of more peaceful years ahead.

I am also—I am also, of course, very thankful to Governor Sarah Palin, one of the best campaigners I've ever seen ... one of the best campaigners I have ever seen, and an impressive new voice in our party for reform and the principles that have always been our greatest strength ... her husband Todd and their five beautiful children ... for their tireless dedication to our cause, and the courage and grace they showed in the rough and tumble of a presidential campaign.

We can all look forward with great interest to her future service to Alaska, the Republican Party and our country.

To all my campaign comrades, from Rick Davis and Steve Schmidt and Mark Salter, to every last volunteer who fought so hard and valiantly, month after month, in what at times seemed to be the most challenged campaign in modern times, thank you so much. A lost election will never mean more to me than the privilege of your faith and friendship.

I don't know—I don't know what more we could have done to try to win this election. I'll leave that to others to determine. Every candidate makes mistakes, and I'm sure I made my share of them. But I won't spend a moment of the future regretting what might have been.

This campaign was and will remain the great honor of my life, and my heart is filled with nothing but gratitude for the experience and to the American people for giving me a fair hearing before deciding that Senator Obama and my old friend Senator Joe Biden should have the honor of leading us for the next four years.

Please. Please (following booing by the crowd).

I would not—I would not be an American worthy of the name should I regret a fate that has allowed me the extraordinary privilege of serving this country for a half a century.

Today, I was a candidate for the highest office in the country I love so much. And tonight, I remain her servant. That is blessing enough for anyone, and I thank the people of Arizona for it.

Tonight—tonight, more than any night, I hold in my heart nothing but love for this country and for all its citizens, whether they supported me or Senator Obama—whether they supported me or Senator Obama.

I wish Godspeed to the man who was my former opponent and will be my president. And I call on all Americans, as I have often in this campaign, to not despair of our present difficulties, but to believe, always, in the promise and greatness of America, because nothing is inevitable here.

Americans never quit. We never surrender.

We never hide from history. We make history.

Thank you, and God bless you, and God bless America. Thank you all very much.

President-Elect Barack Obama:

Speech on Winning the

General Election

Election Night

Chicago, IL

November 04, 2008

If there is anyone out there who still doubts that America is a place where all things are possible; who still wonders if the dream of our founders is alive in our time; who still questions the power of our democracy, tonight is your answer.

It's the answer told by lines that stretched around schools and churches in numbers this nation has never seen; by people who waited three hours and four hours, many for the very first time in their lives, because they believed that this time must be different; that their voice could be that difference.

It's the answer spoken by young and old, rich and poor, Democrat and Republican, black, white, Latino, Asian, Native American, gay, straight, disabled and not disabled—Americans who sent a message to the world that we have never been a collection of Red States and Blue States: we are, and always will be, the United States of America.

It's the answer that led those who have been told for so long by so many to be cynical, and fearful, and doubtful of what we can achieve to put their hands on the arc of history and bend it once more toward the hope of a better day.

It's been a long time coming, but tonight, because of what we did on this day, in this election, at this defining moment, change has come to America.

I just received a very gracious call from Senator McCain. He fought long and hard in this campaign, and he's fought even longer and harder for the country he loves. He has endured sacrifices for America that most of us cannot begin to imagine, and we are better off for the service rendered by this brave and selfless leader. I congratulate him and Governor Palin for all they have achieved, and I look forward to working with them to renew this nation's promise in the months ahead.

I want to thank my partner in this journey, a man who campaigned from his heart and spoke for the men and women he grew up with on the streets of Scranton and rode with on that train home to Delaware, the Vice President-elect of the United States, Joe Biden.

I would not be standing here tonight without the unyielding support of my best friend for the last sixteen years, the rock of our family and the love of my life, our nation's next First Lady, Michelle Obama. Sasha and Malia, I love you both so much, and you have earned the new puppy that's coming with us to the White House. And while she's no longer with us, I know my grandmother is watching, along with the family that made me who I am. I miss them tonight, and know that my debt to them is beyond measure.

To my campaign manager David Plouffe, my chief strategist David Axelrod, and the best campaign team ever assembled in the history of politics—you made this happen, and I am forever grateful for what you've sacrificed to get it done.

But above all, I will never forget who this victory truly belongs to—it belongs to you.

I was never the likeliest candidate for this office. We didn't start with much money or many endorsements. Our campaign was not hatched in the halls of Washington—it began in the backyards of Des Moines and the living rooms of Concord and the front porches of Charleston.

It was built by working men and women who dug into what little savings they had to give five dollars and ten dollars and twenty dollars to this cause. It grew strength from the young people who rejected the myth of their generation's apathy; who left their homes and their families for jobs that offered little pay and less sleep; from the not-so-young people who braved the bitter cold and scorching heat to knock on the doors of perfect strangers; from the millions of Americans who volunteered, and organized, and proved that more than two centuries later, a government of the people, by the people and for the people has not perished from this Earth. This is your victory.

I know you didn't do this just to win an election and I know you didn't do it for me. You did it because you understand the enormity of the task that lies ahead. For even as we celebrate tonight, we know the challenges that tomorrow will bring are the greatest of our lifetime—two wars, a planet in peril, the worst financial crisis in a century. Even as we stand here tonight, we know there are brave Americans waking up in the deserts of Iraq and the mountains of Afghanistan to risk their lives for us. There are mothers and fathers who will lie awake after their children fall asleep and wonder how they'll make the mortgage, or pay their doctor's bills, or save enough for college. There is new energy to harness and new jobs to be created; new schools to build and threats to meet and alliances to repair.

The road ahead will be long. Our climb will be steep. We may not get there in one year or even one term, but America—I have never been more hopeful than I am tonight that we will get there. I promise you—we as a people will get there.

There will be setbacks and false starts. There are many who won't agree with every decision or policy I make as President, and we know that government can't solve every problem. But I will always be honest with you about the challenges we face. I will listen to you, especially when we disagree. And above all, I will ask you join in the work of remaking this nation the only way it's been done in America for two-hundred and twenty-one years—block by block, brick by brick, calloused hand by calloused hand.

What began twenty-one months ago in the depths of winter must not end on this autumn night. This victory alone is not the change we seek—it is only the chance for us to make that change. And that cannot happen if we go back to the way things were. It cannot happen without you.

So let us summon a new spirit of patriotism; of service and responsibility where each of us resolves to pitch in and work harder and look after not only ourselves, but each other. Let us remember that if this financial crisis taught us anything, it's that we cannot have a thriving Wall Street while Main Street suffers—in this country, we rise or fall as one nation; as one people.

Let us resist the temptation to fall back on the same partisanship and pettiness and immaturity that has poisoned our politics for so long. Let us remember that it was a man from this state who first carried the banner of the Republican Party to the White House—a party founded on the values of self-reliance, individual liberty, and national unity. Those are values we all share, and while the Democratic Party has won a great victory tonight, we do so with a measure of humility and determination to heal the divides that have held back our progress. As Lincoln said to a nation far more divided than ours, "We are not enemies, but friends... though passion may have strained it must not break our bonds of affection." And to those Americans whose support I have yet to earn—I may not have won your vote, but I hear your voices, I need your help, and I will be your President too.

And to all those watching tonight from beyond our shores, from parliaments and palaces to those who are huddled around radios in the forgotten corners of our world—our stories are singular, but our destiny is shared, and a new dawn of American leadership is at hand. To those who would tear this world down—we will defeat you. To those who seek peace and security—we support you. And to all those who have wondered if America's beacon still burns as bright—tonight we proved once more that the true strength of our nation comes not from our the might of our arms or the scale of our wealth, but from the enduring power of our ideals: democracy, liberty, opportunity, and unyielding hope.

For that is the true genius of America—that America can change. Our union can be perfected. And what we have already achieved gives us hope for what we can and must achieve tomorrow.

This election had many firsts and many stories that will be told for generations. But one that's on my mind tonight is about a woman who cast her ballot in Atlanta. She's a lot like the millions of others who stood in line to make their voice heard in this election except for one thing—Ann Nixon Cooper is 106 years old.

She was born just a generation past slavery; a time when there were no cars on the road or planes in the sky; when someone like her couldn't vote for two reasons—because she was a woman and because of the color of her skin.

And tonight, I think about all that she's seen throughout her century in America—the heartache and the hope; the struggle and the progress; the times we were told that we can't, and the people who pressed on with that American creed: Yes we can.

At a time when women's voices were silenced and their hopes dismissed, she lived to see them stand up and speak out and reach for the ballot. Yes we can.

When there was despair in the dust bowl and depression across the land, she saw a nation conquer fear itself with a New Deal, new jobs and a new sense of common purpose. Yes we can.

When the bombs fell on our harbor and tyranny threatened the world, she was there to witness a generation rise to greatness and a democracy was saved. Yes we can.

She was there for the buses in Montgomery, the hoses in Birmingham, a bridge in Selma, and a preacher from Atlanta who told a people that "We Shall Overcome." Yes we can.

A man touched down on the moon, a wall came down in Berlin, a world was connected by our own science and imagination. And this year, in this election, she touched her finger to a screen, and cast her vote, because after 106 years in America, through the best of times and the darkest of hours, she knows how America can change. Yes we can.

America, we have come so far. We have seen so much. But there is so much more to do. So tonight, let us ask ourselves—if our children should live to see the next century; if my daughters should be so lucky to live as long as Ann Nixon Cooper, what change will they see? What progress will we have made?

This is our chance to answer that call. This is our moment. This is our time—to put our people back to work and open doors of opportunity for our kids; to restore prosperity and promote the cause of peace; to reclaim the American Dream and reaffirm that fundamental truth—that out of many, we are one; that while we breathe, we hope, and where we are met with cynicism, and doubt, and those who tell us that we can't, we will respond with that timeless creed that sums up the spirit of a people:

Yes We Can. Thank you, God bless you, and may God Bless the United States of America.

Context

✿

President George W. Bush:
Comment on Elections

The White House,

Washington, DC

November 5, 2008

$\mathcal{G}$ood morning. Last night, I had a warm conversation with President-elect Barack Obama. I congratulated him and Senator Biden on their impressive victory. I told the President-elect he can count on complete cooperation from my administration as he makes the transition to the White House.

I also spoke to Senator John McCain. I congratulated him on a determined campaign that he and Governor Palin ran. The American people will always be grateful for the lifetime of service John McCain has devoted to this nation. And I know he'll continue to make tremendous contributions to our country.

No matter how they cast their ballots, all Americans can be proud of the history that was made yesterday. Across the country, citizens voted in large numbers. They showed a watching world the vitality of America's democracy, and the strides we have made toward a more perfect union. They chose a President whose journey represents a triumph of the American story—a testament to hard work, optimism, and faith in the enduring promise of our nation.

Many of our citizens thought they would never live to see that day. This moment is especially uplifting for a generation of Americans who witnessed the struggle for civil rights with their own eyes—and four decades later see a dream fulfilled.

A long campaign has now ended, and we move forward as one nation. We're embarking on a period of change in Washington, yet there are some things that will not change. The United States government will stay vigilant in meeting its most important responsibility—protecting the American people. And the world can be certain this commitment will remain steadfast under our next Commander-in-Chief.

There's important work to do in the months ahead, and I will continue to conduct the people's business as long as this office remains in my trust. During this time of transition, I will keep the President-elect fully informed on important decisions. And when the time comes on January the 20th, Laura and I will return home to Texas with treasured memories of our time here—and with profound gratitude for the honor of serving this amazing country.

It will be a stirring sight to watch President Obama, his wife, Michelle, and their beautiful girls step through the doors of the White House. I know millions of Americans will be overcome with pride at this inspiring moment that so many have awaited so long. I know Senator Obama's beloved mother and grandparents would have been thrilled to watch the child they raised ascend the steps of the Capitol—and take his oath to uphold the Constitution of the greatest nation on the face of the earth.

Last night I extended an invitation to the President-elect and Mrs. Obama to come to the White House. And Laura and I are looking forward to welcoming them as soon as possible.

Thank you very much.

Appendix A

The Emancipation Proclamation

September 22, 1862

A Transcription

By the President of the
United States of America.

A Proclamation.

I, Abraham Lincoln, President of the United States of America, and Commander-in-Chief of the Army and Navy thereof, do hereby proclaim and declare that hereafter, as heretofore, the war will be prosecuted for the object of practically restoring the constitutional relation between the United States, and each of the States, and the people thereof, in which States that relation is, or may be, suspended or disturbed.

That it is my purpose, upon the next meeting of Congress to again recommend the adoption of a practical measure tendering pecuniary aid to the free acceptance or rejection of all slave States, so called, the people whereof may not then be in rebellion against the United States and which States may then have voluntarily adopted, or thereafter may voluntarily adopt, immediate or gradual abolishment of slavery within their respective limits; and that the effort to colonize persons of African descent, with their consent, upon this continent, or elsewhere, with the previously obtained consent of the Governments existing there, will be continued.

That on the first day of January in the year of our Lord, one thousand eight hundred and sixty-three, all persons held as slaves within any State, or designated part of a State, the people whereof shall then be in rebellion against the United States shall be then, thenceforward, and forever free; and the executive government of the United States, including the military and naval authority thereof, will recognize and maintain the freedom of such persons, and will do no act or acts to repress such persons, or any of them, in any efforts they may make for their actual freedom.

That the executive will, on the first day of January aforesaid, by proclamation, designate the States, and part of States, if any, in which the people thereof respectively, shall then be in rebellion against the United States; and the fact that any State, or the people thereof shall, on that day be, in good faith represented in the Congress of the United States, by members chosen thereto, at elections wherein a majority of the qualified voters of such State shall have participated, shall, in the absence of strong countervailing testimony, be deemed conclusive evidence that such State and the people thereof, are not then in rebellion against the United States.

That attention is hereby called to an Act of Congress entitled "An Act to make an additional Article of War" approved March 13, 1862, and which act is in the words and figure following:

"Be it enacted by the Senate and House of Representatives of the United States of America in Congress assembled, That hereafter the following shall be promulgated as an additional article of war for the government of the army of the United States, and shall be obeyed and observed as such:

"Article-All officers or persons in the military or naval service of the United States are prohibited from employing any of the forces under their respective commands for the purpose of returning fugitives from service or labor, who may have escaped from any persons to whom such service or labor is claimed to be due, and any officer who shall be found guilty by a court martial of violating this article shall be dismissed from the service.

"Sec.2. And be it further enacted, That this act shall take effect from and after its passage."

Also to the ninth and tenth sections of an act entitled "An Act to suppress Insurrection, to punish Treason and Rebellion, to seize and confiscate property of rebels, and for other purposes," approved July 17, 1862, and which sections are in the words and figures following:

"Sec.9. And be it further enacted, That all slaves of persons who shall hereafter be engaged in rebellion against the government of the United States, or who shall in any way give aid or comfort thereto, escaping from such persons and taking refuge within the lines of the army; and all slaves captured from such persons or deserted by them and coming under the control of the government of the United States; and all slaves of such persons found on (or) being within any place occupied by rebel forces and afterwards occupied by the forces of the United States, shall be deemed captives of war, and shall be forever free of their servitude and not again held as slaves.

"Sec.10. And be it further enacted, That no slave escaping into any State, Territory, or the District of Columbia, from any other State, shall be delivered up, or in any way impeded or hindered of his liberty, except for crime, or some offence against the laws, unless the person claiming said fugitive shall first make oath that the person to whom the labor or service of such fugitive is alleged to be due is his lawful owner, and has not borne arms against the United States in the present rebellion, nor in any way given aid and comfort thereto; and no person engaged in the military or naval service of the United States shall, under any pretence whatever, assume to decide on the validity of the claim of any person to the service or labor of any other person, or surrender up any such person to the claimant, on pain of being dismissed from the service."

And I do hereby enjoin upon and order all persons engaged in the military and naval service of the United States to observe, obey, and enforce, within their respective spheres of service, the act, and sections above recited.

And the executive will in due time recommend that all citizens of the United States who shall have remained loyal thereto throughout the rebellion, shall (upon the restoration of the constitutional relation between the United States, and their respective States, and people, if that relation shall have been suspended or disturbed) be compensated for all losses by acts of the United States, including the loss of slaves.

In witness whereof, I have hereunto set my hand, and caused the seal of the United States to be affixed.

Done at the City of Washington this twenty-second day of September, in the year of our Lord, one thousand, eight hundred and sixty-two, and of the Independence of the United States the eighty seventh.

[Signed:]
Abraham Lincoln
By the President

[Signed:]
William H. Seward
Secretary of State

Appendix B
The Thirteenth Amendment

(Adopted December 6, 1865)

& the
Fourteenth Amendment

(Adopted July 9, 1868)

to the
United States Constitution

Thirteenth Amendment

Section 1. Neither slavery nor involuntary servitude, except as a punishment for crime where of the party shall have been duly convicted, shall exist within the United States, or any place subject to their jurisdiction.

Section 2. Congress shall have the power to enforce this article by appropriate legislation.

Fourteenth Amendment

Section 1. All persons born or naturalized in the United States, and subject to the jurisdiction thereof, are citizens of the United States and of the State wherein they reside. No State shall make or enforce any law which shall abridge the privileges or immunities of citizens of the United States; nor shall any State deprive any person of life, liberty, or property, without due process of law; nor deny to any person within its jurisdiction the equal protection of the laws.

Section 2. Representatives shall be apportioned among the several States according to their respective numbers, counting the whole number of persons in each State, excluding Indians not taxed. But when the right to vote at any election for the choice of electors for President and Vice President of the United States, Representatives in Congress, the Executive and Judicial officers of a State, or the members of the Legislature thereof, is denied to any of the male inhabitants of such State, being twenty-one years of age, and citizens of the United States, or in any way abridged, except for participation in rebellion, or other crime, the basis of representation therein shall be reduced in the proportion which the number of such male citizens shall bear to the whole number of male citizens twenty-one years of age in such State.

Section 3. No one shall be a Senator or Representative in Congress, or elector of President and Vice President, or hold any office, civil or military, under the United States, or under any State, who, having previously taken an oath, as a member of Congress, or as an officer of the United States, or as a member of any State legislature, or as an executive or judicial officer of any State, to support the Constitution of the United States, shall have engaged in insurrection or rebellion against the same, or given aid or comfort to the enemies thereof. But Congress may by a vote of two-thirds of each House, remove such disability.

Section 4. The validity of the public debt of the United States, authorized by law, including debts incurred for payment of pensions and bounties for services in suppressing insurrection or rebellion, shall not be questioned. But neither the United States nor any State shall assume or pay any debt or obligation incurred in aid of insurrection or rebellion against the United States, or any claim for the loss or emancipation of any slave; but all such debts, obligations and claims shall be held illegal and void.

Section 5. The Congress shall have power to enforce, by appropriate legislation, the provisions of this article.

Appendix C
The Obama Family

Immediate Family

Barack Obama, born August 4, 1961 in Honolulu, Hawaii
Michelle Obama, nee Robinson (wife), born January 17, 1964 in Chicago, Illinois
Malia Obama (daughter), born 1998 in Chicago, Illinois
Sasha Obama (daughter), born 2001 in Chicago, Illinois

Extended Family-Maternal

Stanley Ann Obama (Ann Obama), nèe Dunham (mother), born 1942, died 1995. (later, S. Ann Dunham Soetoro and then Ann Dunham Sutoro).
Madelyn Lee Dunham nèe Payne (grandmother), born 1922 in Peru, Kansas; died 2008
Stanley Armour Dunham (grandfather), born 1918 in Augusta, Kansas; died 1992

Charles T. Payne (great uncle), born 1925
Maya Soetoro-Ng (half-sister) born 1970 (Indonesia)
Konrad Ng (brother in law, married to Maya Soetoro Ng), born 1974 (Canada)

Extended Family-Paternal

Barack Obama Sr. (father), born 1936 (Kenya), died 1982

KEY SPEECHES OF PRESIDENT-ELECT BARACK OBAMA

Abo Obama (half-brother), born 1968
Auma Obama (half-sister), born 1960
Bernard Obama (half-brother), born 1970
David Ndesandjo (half-brother) (deceased)
George Hussein Onyango Obama (half brother), born 1982
Habiba Akumu Obama (grandmother)
Hussein Onyango Obama (grandfather), born 1895 (Kenya), died 1979
Kezia Obama (setp-mother), born 1940
Malik Obama (half-brother), born 1958
Mark Ndesandjo (half-brother)
Omar Obama (half-uncle), born 1944
Ruth Ndesandjo (step-mother), probably born during the 1940s
Said Obama (half uncle), probably born during the 1950s
Sarah Obama (step-grandmother), born 1922
Yusuf Obama (half uncle), probably born during the 1950s
Zeituni Onyango (half sister), born 1952

www.ingramcontent.com/pod-product-compliance
Lightning Source LLC
Chambersburg PA
CBHW021541260326
41914CB00001B/108